SECOND ED

20th CENTURY RUSSIA

THE SEARCH FOR POWER AND AUTHORITY

GRAEME GILL

Withdrawn

NELSON

THOMSON LEARNING

Australia · Canada · Mexico · Singapore · Spain · United Kingdom · United States

NELSON

TM

THOMSON LEARNING

First Published 1994
10 9 8 7 6 5 4 3
03 02 01 00
Copyright © Graeme Gill 1994

The acknowledgments on p. vi constitute an extension of this copyright notice.

National Library of Australia
Cataloguing-in-Publication data

Gill, Graeme J.
  Twentieth century Russia.

  2nd ed.
  Bibliography.
  Includes index.
  ISBN 0 17 008991 6.

  1. Soviet Union – History. 2. Soviet Union – Politics and government. 3. Russia – History – 20th century. 4. Russia – Politics and government – 20th century. I. Title (Series: Nelson modern history series).

947.08

Designed by R.T.J. Klinkhamer
Cover design by Erika Budiman
Cover photographs: Sergei Chekhonin, cover for John Reed's *Ten Days that Shook the World*, 1923, courtesy of Aurora Art Publishers, St Petersburg; Fyoder Shurpin, 'Morning of our Motherland', State Tretiakov Gallery, courtesy of Art Publishing House, Moscow.
Typeset in 10/13 pt Trump Mediaeval by Post Typesetters
Printed in China

Nelson Australia Pty Limited ACN 004 603 454 (incorporated in Victoria) trading as Thomas Nelson Australia.

The I (T) P trademark is used under licence.

Within the publishing process Thomas Nelson Australia uses resources, technology and suppliers that are as environment friendly as possible.

CONTENTS

ACKNOWLEDGEMENTS

For permission to reproduce copyright photographs and art work the author and publisher would like to thank:

Mrs G. Allen, pp. 36-7; Archiv Gerstenberg, p. 10; BBC Hulton Picture Library, pp. 62 (bottom), 95; Camera Press, p. 150; Mary Evans/Alexander Meledin Collection, pp. 40, 76; John Freeman, p. 149; Gorskii, *Photographs for the Tsar*, p. 2 (right); Russian Pictorial Collection, Hoover Institution Archives, pp. 20, 35; Hulton Deutsch, pp. 14; Imperial War Museum, p. 67; David King Collection, p. 43; Life Picture Service, p. 122; Mansell Collection, pp. 2 (left), 99; Museum of Modern Art, Oxford, pp. 83, 114; New York Public Library, pp. 9, 44, 62 (top), 124; Novosti Press Agency, Moscow, p. 6; Popperfoto, p. 131; Society for Co-operation in Russian and Soviet Studies (SCR), pp. 90, 108, 116 (bottom), 152; Sovietsky Khudoznik Publishers, pp. 57, 69, 82, 85, 87, 93, 113, 116 (top), 121, 130, 144, 146; Staatsbibliothek, p. 128; Suddeutscher Verlag, p. 167; TASS from Sovfoto, p. 170; UPI/Bettman, pp. 11, 18, 28, 29, 45, 64, 74, 126, 147, 169; Victoria and Albert Museum, pp. 4, 5; L. Volkov-Lannit, *Istorii pishetsia ob'ektivom*, p. 47; Warder Collection, p. 94.

For permission to reproduce copyright material the author and publisher would like to thank the following:

Bone, A. (ed.), *The Bolsheviks and the October Revolution: Central Committee Minutes of the Russian Social Democratic Labour Party (Bolsheviks) August 1917–February 1918*, Pluto Press, London, 1974, pp. 48–53; Clarke, R.A. & Matko, D.J.I., *Soviet Economic Facts, 1917–18*, London, Macmillan, 1983, pp. 111, 115, 146, 153; McCauley, M. (ed.), *The Russian Revolution and the Soviet State 1917–1921, Documents*, Macmillan, London, 1975, p. 66; Sholokhov, M., *Virgin Soil Upturned*, Penguin, Harmondsworth, 1977, pp. 109–110; Spector, I., *The First Russian Revolution: its impact on Asia*, Prentice Hall, Englewood Cliffs, 1962, pp. 9–10.

PREFACE

THIS IS A HISTORY, written for senior secondary school students, of Russia/ the Soviet Union from 1900 until the death of Stalin in 1953. It traces the transformation of what in 1900 was an underdeveloped, traditional, autocratic, monarchical Russia (albeit with some developed sectors) into a developed, modern, authoritarian, republican Soviet Union (albeit with some undeveloped sectors). The principal themes of the study are the search for power and authority. There are two main arenas for the interplay of these themes: the society at large and the structure of the regime itself.

Simply put, power is the ability to get one's way. Authority is that quality whereby people obey because they believe that the person or institution giving orders has a right to give those orders and they have a corresponding duty to obey. Power and authority do not always go together, but the exercise of power is likely to be much more stable if it is buttressed by authority. In the arena of the society at large, this study shows the way in which tsarist authority evaporated, fundamentally undermining its ability to exercise sufficient power to sustain itself. When the Bolsheviks took over the government of Russia, they had to build up both their authority in the eyes of the populace and their capacity to exercise effective power over the lands they claimed. Within the structure of the regime, the questions of power and authority related both to the construction of stable patterns of relationships between political institutions and the role of individual political leaders.

Of course, these themes are not the only ones that could be used to order the study of Russian history. My justification for using them as the organising principles is that in an important respect they are primary; in Russia and the Soviet Union, the power relationships between the regime and society and within the regime have been crucial in structuring not just the course of elite politics, but also the lives of the ordinary citizenry. Even those subjects favoured by social historians have been heavily influenced by political factors (and vice versa), as I have tried to show in this book. Nevertheless there are clearly gaps in the account; the size of the book alone ensured that this would be the case. I hope, however, that the use of these themes has enabled the account that has emerged to be coherent and sufficiently full for the purposes for which it has been produced. The questions at the beginning of each chapter have been designed both to raise issues related to these themes and to signal some areas which, while not fitting neatly into these themes, are worthy of consideration.

Dates cited are those which applied at the time. Until February 1918, Russia followed the Julian calendar which, in the twentieth century, was thirteen days behind the Gregorian calendar used in the West.

The term 'Russia' in the title is, strictly speaking, incorrect. The Russian republic was only one of 15 constituent republics of the Union of Soviet Socialist Republics. Russia has nevertheless been employed in line with popular usage and for simplicity's sake. Its use is in no way meant to deny the ethnic individuality of the non-Russian groups in what was the Soviet population.

This second edition is considerably larger than the first. It contains four new case studies and considerably more statistical material. The text has been almost completely reworked, and suggested activities have been added to each chapter to highlight specific issues. In this regard, I would like to thank those teachers whose comments were instrumental in structuring this reworking.

ABBREVIATIONS AND ACRONYMS

CC	Central Committee
Cheka	All-Russian Extraordinary Commission for Combating Counter-Revolution, Sabotage and Speculation. Established December 1917, replaced by GPU, 1922.
GKO	State Defence Committee
GPU	State Political Directorate. Established 1922, replaced by OGPU in 1924.
NEP	New Economic Policy
NKVD	People's Commissariat of Internal Affairs. Absorbed OGPU 1934.
OGPU	Unified State Political Directorate. Established 1924, absorbed by NKVD 1934.
RCP(b)	Russian Communist Party (Bolsheviks) (party's name from 1918–25)
RSFSR	Russian Soviet Federated Socialist Republic
Sovnarkom	Council of People's Commissars
SRs	Socialist Revolutionaries
Stavka	General Headquarters, Supreme Command

THE TWILIGHT OF IMPERIAL RUSSIA

THE LAST YEARS of imperial Russia were, in retrospect, characterised by an important paradox. Externally, Russia appeared very strong. There had been substantial economic growth and her military force was large. But internally she was weak, with an inflexible political structure and a society undergoing dramatic change.

Focus questions

The following questions provide a focus for studying this chapter:
- How stable was the social basis of tsarist rule?
- Why was the government unable to meet the challenges emerging in the first decade and a half of this century?
- How important were the Bolsheviks before 1917?
- What effect did World War I have on the tsarist government?

THE AMBIGUITIES OF TSARIST POWER

At the beginning of the twentieth century tsarist rule seemed as secure as it had ever been. Largely under the influence of Finance Minister Witte (1892–1903), Russia had embarked on a serious program of industrialisation. With this growing industrial strength came military strength, and a more important role on the international stage. Domestically, within Russia, the government seemed little troubled. Despite the assassination of Tsar Alexander II in 1881, the revolutionary movement that had developed in the second half of the nineteenth century seemed to pose no threat to the authorities. While there were some industrial troubles and spontaneous disturbances in the countryside, few questioned the stability of the tsarist system. As the Romanov dynasty approached its tercentenary on the throne in 1913, there was little outward sign that barely four years later it would be swept from power by popular revolution.

In fact, the Russian political structure was far shakier than it appeared. Many observers were taken in by the imposing structure of tsarist rule and failed to see the serious weaknesses within. As a political structure, it seemed invulnerable. At the turn of the century the tsar was still the supreme autocrat and ruler of all the Russias, formally unlimited by any constitutional provisions aimed at restricting his power. All government ministers were appointed by him and held office at his pleasure. Government bodies were purely advisory. The all-powerful tsar had a large bureaucracy to do his bidding. The quality of the bureaucracy had improved immensely during the nineteenth century as it became more professional, and by the turn of the century it seemed to be a moderately efficient instrument of rule.

Nicholas and Alexandra in traditional Russian costume at the time of the tercentenary celebrations of the Romanov dynasty, 1913 (Mansell Collection)

Religion was a central part of Russian life. This is symbolised by the church on the hill surrounded by the village. However, the religious commitment of most of the population seems to have been stronger with regard to ritual than to doctrine. Nevertheless, the village priest was often an influential figure (Gorskii, Photographs for the Tsar)

Discuss

• What symbolism is conveyed by the comparative placement of the church and the houses in the picture on p.2?

This institutional structure was reinforced symbolically by the church and physically by the military. The Russian Orthodox Church was effectively an arm of the state. Its governing body, the Holy Synod, was chosen by the tsar and his advisers rather than by the church itself. The church gave legitimacy to the tsarist system and provided a symbolic prop for the structure as a whole. The huge army and the growing naval fleet were manned through universal conscription. The military provided the coercive power that the tsarist system, like all political systems, needed to maintain its power and position. But despite these apparent sources of strength, the tsarist system had a serious weakness: the fragility of its social basis.

Traditional autocracies usually rely for their social support on the established landed class, the nobility. Those pursuing a path of modernisation often also look for support to the middle classes, particularly the entrepreneurial groups that are so important to that process. In turn-of-the-century Russia, both classes were very weak.

The Nobility

The source of the weakness of the noble landowning class lay in the nature of its relationship with the land.

An initial problem for the nobility was the lack of concentration of their lands. When the tsars distributed the land to the nobles, they wanted to ensure that landowners couldn't consolidate their holdings into solid territorial bases. So the nobility were given small parcels of land across the length and breadth of Russia. The effect of this was reinforced by the absence of laws of entail and primogeniture. This ensured that when land was passed from one generation to the next, rather than being passed intact to the eldest son (primogeniture), it was divided between all the sons. The size of individual holdings therefore decreased over the generations.

Furthermore, there was little incentive for landowners to improve agricultural techniques and thereby overcome the technical and climatic barriers to producing a consistent agricultural surplus. The institution of serfdom, which was enforced by the state, provided landowners with a cheap labour force that enabled them to avoid serious agricultural innovation. When the serfs were liberated in 1861 and the landowners lost their captive labour force, many nobles were unable to farm their lands profitably. In response, many sold off their holdings. Unlike in England, noble landowners did not seek to improve their economic position by entering state service. Very few nobles entered the bureaucracy; prior to 1914, some 80 per cent of posts in the top four grades

The shortness of the growing season has always been a major problem for Russian agriculture. The severity of the winter, when animals had to live inside with the peasants, is shown in this picture of a peasant hut in mid-winter (Victoria & Albert Museum, London)

of the bureaucracy were filled by people who did not come from the noble landowning class. As the nineteenth century drew to a close, the landowners were a weak and declining force in Russian society.

The Middle Class

The inability of a strong, entrepreneurial middle class to develop in Russia was also largely due to economic factors. Individual farmers could not produce consistent, sizeable agricultural surpluses. This hindered their ability to accumulate sufficient capital to invest in commercial and industrial development. Again unlike in England, there were few opportunities for large numbers of individual entrepreneurs to emerge to foster development. Instead the Russian state played a very large part in fostering industrial development. So did foreign investment. But by responding in this way to the lack of entrepreneurial development, the state was further restricting such development. The resources the state used to promote industrial growth were effectively resources denied to the private sector. Consequently, entrepreneurs in Russia generally grew up in the shadow of the state, and when they undertook business activities, it was often with the assistance of state subsidies and behind tariff walls. A strong, entrepreneurial middle class independent of the state did not exist.

   Two other classes were of fundamental importance at this time, the peasantry and the working class.

PROBLEMS AND ISSUES
● Modernisation

The Peasantry

The peasants were by far the biggest group in the country — rural dwellers were still 86 per cent of the population in 1914 — and at the turn of the century they harboured serious resentments. Although peasants had been freed by the Emancipation Act of 1861, they had gained neither all the land to which they believed they were entitled, nor obtained it without payment. Through a system of periodic redemption payments, peasants were forced to buy land they believed rightfully belonged to them and which they may have worked as serfs for generations. By the end of the nineteenth century, a large number had fallen behind in their payments and were in serious debt. For many peasants, particularly in the central agricultural region, the land they received at the time of emancipation was actually less than they had had prior to 1861.

Most peasants continued to live in the peasant commune, an organisational structure which governed their lives. One of the chief functions of the commune was periodically to redistribute the land among households on the basis of changing family size. This meant that peasant land was subject to the same splintering process as the land of the noble landowners. The commune also ensured the continued dominance of archaic agricultural methods, and therefore inefficient farming, in many parts of Russia. This picture of a declining peasantry was not uniform across Russia. In some areas peasant agriculture prospered, particularly in new agricultural regions where the commune was not established and where private farms predominated. For many peasants, the half century following emancipation was one of continuing misery and poverty.

There were no serious peasant disturbances during this period. One reason for this is that one of the sustaining myths of the tsarist system remained

Life in the village was controlled by the skhod *or assembly of elders. This meeting occurred in 1910 (Victoria & Albert Museum, London)*

intact. Deeply embedded in peasant folklore was the belief in the *batiushka tsar*, the 'little father'. It was widely believed that the tsar was deeply concerned for the peasants' welfare and continually looking after their interests. If new policies harmed the peasants and their interests, peasants blamed the tsar's advisers for misleading him. Indeed, many earlier peasant revolts had been mounted in the name of the 'just tsar': attempts to throw out the advisers and restore the organic relationship between people and tsar. While this personalised view of legitimate authority remained dominant, it was a powerful prop to tsarist stability.

The Working Class

PROBLEMS AND ISSUES
● Modernisation

The difficulties encountered by much peasant agriculture in the last half of the nineteenth century contributed to the flow of peasants into the cities in search of work. The flow into the cities was increased by the government policy of maximising agricultural surpluses to fund industrial development. The growth of industry was accompanied by the emergence of an urban problem. As happened in other countries, the early stages of the industrial revolution in Russia produced very harsh living and working conditions. Long hours, inadequate safety precautions, harsh factory discipline, low wages, crowded housing, no social services or insurance and few health regulations made life a misery for many Russian factory workers. Trade unions were illegal, so workers were hampered in their attempts to organise to defend their interests. In

Living quarters for workers in the big cities were cramped and squalid. Many families, such as the one pictured, lived in workers' hostels (Novosti)

addition, many Russian factories were large, much bigger than their counterparts in the West; in 1914, 40 per cent of urban workers were in plants of more than a thousand workers. The size of the factories contributed to the workers' sense of alienation. Many sought to combat this by forming associations of people from the same region, the *zemliachestvo*. Indeed, a continuing connection to the land and the home village was a major characteristic of the Russian working class at this time. Although working full time in the factory, many workers returned home for family festivals and in the late summer to help with the harvesting. Many workers were first generation peasants and, although sections of the workforce were a hardened proletariat, most retained much of their peasant outlook.

Review

• Draw a diagram showing the relationship between the different classes and the monarchy in tsarist Russia.

INDUSTRIALISATION AND ITS CONSEQUENCES

PROBLEMS AND ISSUES

• Modernisation

Towards the end of the nineteenth century, the Russian government once again became concerned about Russia falling behind its European rivals. For security reasons, the government felt that Russia had to speed up industrial development and thereby strengthen its defences. The attempt to increase the tempo of industrial development had begun in 1861, but under the influence of Sergei Witte it was dramatically accelerated in the two and a half decades before the war.

The main impetus for industrial development at this time came from government policy. There were four main components of this policy:

• High tariff walls to provide protection for Russian industry against cheaper competition from abroad.
• Increased grain exports to provide capital for investment and to guarantee foreign loans.
• Foreign loans as a source of investment capital.
• Railway construction to improve the economic infrastructure and stimulate heavy industry, which produced the requirements for railway expansion (e.g. engines, tracks).

M.E. Falkus, *The Industrialisation of Russia: 1700–1914*, London, Macmillan, 1972, p.46

Chiefly as a result of government stimulus, industrial development accelerated. According to one study, the average annual rate of growth of industrial production increased as shown in Table 1.1.

Table 1.1 Growth of Industrial Production

1890–99	8.03%
1900–06	1.43%
1907–13	6.25%

The growth in industrial production is also clearly reflected in gross output figures (in 000 tonnes):

Adapted from Roger Weiss, (ed.), *Russian Economic History. The Nineteenth Century*, Chicago, University of Chicago Press, 1989, p.69

Table 1.2   Growth in Gross Output Figures

	1885	1890	1895	1900	1905	1910	1913
Coal	4338	6111	9246	16 413	18 967	25 400	36 617
Oil	1829	3759	6274	10 505	7590	9794	9347
Pig iron	538	945	1473	2977	2774	3089	4704
Sugar	345	411	538	808	869	1046	1880

In agriculture the picture was not as rosy. The increase in agricultural production over this time barely kept ahead of population growth.

Weiss, *Russian Economic History*, p.69

Table 1.3   Population Growth and Grain Production

	1895	1900	1905	1910	1913
Population (in millions)	123.9	132.9	143.9	160.7	170.9
Grain production (50 districts of European Russia)	43.9	48.3	48.9	60.5	69.4

Over this period grain production increased by 58.1 per cent, while the population grew by 37.9 per cent. There was, therefore, an imbalance in the course of economic development, with industrial development proceeding much further and faster than agriculture.

The policy of rapid industrial development had significant social effects. The most important was the low living standards that accompanied it. The effect of government industrialisation policies was to increase taxes and, through tariffs, raise prices. In addition, the government's policy of increasing grain exports meant increased government acquisition of grain. In turn this meant decreased consumption for the peasants, and resulted in famine in some regions in the 1890s. This pressure on peasant living standards, added to the lack of land and increasing indebtedness, forced many peasants to seek employment in the towns. Peasants gave up the difficulties of the village for the harsh conditions of factory life.

THE 1905 REVOLUTION

The difficult conditions faced by both workers and peasants created a potentially dangerous situation for the government. This potential was realised when the Russian economy experienced a depression in the early twentieth century. Wage reductions and growth in unemployment led to increased strike activity. In the countryside peasant disturbances increased. Peasants reacted to the

A political poster commemorating 'Bloody Sunday', 9 January 1905, when the tsar's troops opened fire on a peaceful demonstration in St Petersburg (New York Public Library)

harsher economic conditions by vigorously pressing their claims for more land, lower taxation, and the abolition of redemption payments. Partly to try to head off this popular discontent, and also to expand Russian influence into Korea, the government led Russia into a war with Japan in 1904. The defeat of the Russian forces provoked revolutionary events that stretched into 1907.

The real starting point for the Revolution was the events of 9 January 1905, which came to be known as 'Bloody Sunday'. A large crowd led by a priest, Father Gapon, and bearing icons and pictures of the tsar marched to the Winter Palace in St Petersburg to present a petition to the tsar. The petition attacked the exploitation of the people by capitalist factory-owners and bureaucrats and demanded a series of measures to redress this. The tone of the petition is reflected in the following extract:

PROBLEMS AND ISSUES

● Revolution

66 We have been enslaved, and enslaved under the auspices of your officials, with their aid, and with their co-operation. Every one of us who has the temerity to raise his voice in defence of the interests of the working class and the people is thrown into jail and sent into exile... All working people and the peasants are at the mercy of the bureaucratic government, comprised of embezzlers of public funds and thieves, who not only disregard the interests of the people, but defy these interests. The bureaucratic government has brought the country to complete ruin, has imposed upon it a disgraceful

war and leads Russia on and on to destruction. We, the workers and the people, have no voice whatsoever in the expenditure of the huge sums extorted from us. We do not even know whither and for what the money collected from the impoverished people goes. The people are deprived of the opportunity to express their wishes and demands, to take part in levying taxes and their expenditure. The workers are deprived of the possibility of organising unions for the protection of their interests.

Sire! Is this in accordance with God's laws, by the grace of which you reign?… This is our last resort. Don't refuse to help your people, lead them out of the grave of disfranchisement, poverty, and ignorance, give them an opportunity to determine their own fate and cast off the unbearable yoke of the bureaucrats. Tear down the wall between you and your people, and let them rule the country with you. You have been placed on the throne for the happiness of the people, but the bureaucrats snatch this happiness from their hands, and it never reaches us. All we get is grief and humiliation. Look without anger, attentively, at our requests, they are not intended for an evil but for a good cause, for both of us, Sire. We do not talk arrogantly, but from a realisation of the necessity to extricate ourselves from a plight unbearable to all of us. Russia is too vast, her needs too diverse and numerous to be run only by bureaucrats. It is necessary to have popular representation, it is necessary that the people help themselves and govern themselves. Only they know their real needs. Do not reject their help; take it; command at once, forthwith, that there be summoned the representatives of the land of Russia from all classes, all strata, including also the representatives of the workers. Let there be a capitalist, a worker, a bureaucrat, a priest, a doctor and a teacher — let them all, whoever they are, elect their own representatives. Let everyone be equal and free in the manner of suffrage and for that purpose command that the elections for the Constituent Assembly be carried out on the basis of universal, secret and equal suffrage. 99

Petition of the Workers and Residents of St Petersburg for Submission to Nicholas II on 9 January 1905, Ivar Spector, *The First Russian Revolution: Its Impact on Asia*, Prentice Hall, Englewood Cliffs, 1962, pp.118–9

Review

- Using this extract from the petition to the tsar, what sort of relationship was believed to exist between ruler and people?
- What were the implications of this relationship for political authority?

This petition clearly blames economic difficulties on those who came between the tsar and the people, and calls on the tsar to knock down the barriers separating him from his subjects. This was an expression of the traditional peasant position, appealing to the 'little father' to help his people and to see past his evil advisers. The petition reflects continuing confidence in the tsar as the source of initiative and change in the system. However, such confidence was shaken by the response: troops opened fire on the crowd, killing many. Although the tsar was not in the Winter Palace at the time and did not order the troops to act in this way, the killing of demonstrators

Women demonstrating in St Petersburg in 1905 (UPI/Bettmann)

dealt a severe blow to the popular image of the tsar and thereby to the major sustaining myth of the tsarist system.

Bloody Sunday stimulated widespread popular unrest in cities and the countryside. In urban centres workers engaged in demonstrations and strikes, sometimes of a very violent character. Workers' organisations began to spring up spontaneously; trade unions emerged and, reluctantly, the government legalised them. Soviets, or workers' councils, emerged in many urban areas as embryonic organs of self-administration. Many soviets developed out of strike committees which grew to take on much wider functions. The most important was in St Petersburg and was dominated by the radical Menshevik (see p.14) Leon Trotsky. Peasant unrest erupted in the countryside on a wide scale in 1905 and 1906. This took the form of land seizure, the destruction of estates and attacks on noble landowners. There was also trouble in the armed forces, with mutinies occurring in various parts of the country.

The October Manifesto

PROBLEMS AND ISSUES

• Revolution

Under pressure from these popular disturbances, in particular the general strike in October 1905 led by the St Petersburg Soviet, the tsar felt compelled to make concessions. He attempted to meet some of the demands of the professional and intelligentsia sections of the population to try to win their support. In the midst of the unrest, the middle class began to press major constitutional demands on the monarch. This group was increasingly politically active in the early years of the century. The most prominent political party representing this group was the Constitutional Democrats, or Kadets, led by Pavel Miliukov. This party called for the establishment of a constitutional monarchy and the summoning of a national assembly.

'The Manifesto of October 17, 1905', George Vernadsky et al (eds), *A Source Book for Russian History from Early Times to 1917: Vol.3 Alexander II to the February Revolution*, Yale University Press, Newhaven, 1972, p.705

The tsar responded to these demands by introducing the October Manifesto in October 1905. The principal stated aim of the Manifesto was to provide the population with the

> ❝ unshakeable foundations of civil liberty on the principles of true inviolability of person, freedom of conscience, speech, assembly and association. ❞

The Manifesto also provided for the State Duma (parliament) to be elected by all classes of the population (significantly widening the franchise) and gave it the right of effective veto over all legislation. The Manifesto split the opposition. Moderates sought to use the Manifesto as a basis for the peaceful reconstruction of Russia and formed themselves into the Octobrist Party. The Kadets wanted to use parliamentary methods in the Duma to expand the concessions granted in the Manifesto in order to achieve a popularly-elected assembly that would draft a new constitution. Both groups were now isolated from the revolutionary parties such as the Bolsheviks and from the St Petersburg Soviet, which rejected the October Manifesto because it granted none of the workers' demands. The tentative alliance that had been emerging between middle-class groups and workers was destroyed. By neutralising criticism from the middle class through granting these concessions, the tsar felt free to crack down with full force on the unruly populace. The urban resistance was broken, and by 1907 unrest in the countryside had been brutally suppressed.

The tsar had used a combination of concession and force to break the revolutionary movement. But this type of response was not enough to stabilise tsarist rule in the long term. It had to be supported by other changes if there was to be any hope for continuing political stability.

The Stolypin Reforms

**PROBLEMS AND ISSUES**

• Counter-revolution

Government ministers recognised the need for change. The main response was the 'wager on the sturdy and the strong' associated with Prime Minister Petr Stolypin (1906–11). This was an attempt to create a class of farmers who owned their own farms and who, through their commitment to private land ownership and the important place they would occupy in the economy, would be a stabilising force in Russian society and a bulwark of support for the tsarist system. This meant making it possible for individual peasants to leave the peasant commune and enclose their land. Over two million homesteads were established under these provisions between 1907 and 1916, mostly in the west and south where the commune was weakest; by 1 May 1915, 14 per cent of communal land was transformed into private land.

It is not certain that the aim behind these provisions, the weakening of the peasant commune, was achieved. More than 80 per cent of members of households remained in the commune and those who separated often retained close links with it. In many areas the resentment caused by departures from the commune may even have strengthened the commitment of continuing members to that institution. There was often jealousy towards those who left. Also, when a departure occurred, redistribution of substantial parts of commune land among its members sometimes resulted in individuals getting poorer quality land than they had had before. In any event, the destruction of 'the separators' in 1917 suggests considerable resentment towards them on the part of those who remained in the commune.

The Duma

The introduction of the Duma was an important change in the political structure, not because it posed any real checks upon the tsar, but because of the arena it provided for public political activity. It was a forum within which the political parties could criticise the government and appeal to the populace in an attempt to build up support. The first Duma met in May 1906. It was dominated by the Kadets, and was far more radical than the government had expected it to be. Accordingly it was dissolved after only two months. The second Duma had stronger representation from both the left and right of the political spectrum and, like the first, was not sympathetic to the government. It was dissolved after four months. In June 1907, the government altered the electoral law in a way that increased the representation of private landowners and the wealthy business sections of society, and substantially reduced that of workers and peasants. This meant that while all major sections of society could gain a voice in the Duma, it would be dominated by 'trustworthy' elements. As a result the third and fourth Dumas were dominated by conservative deputies and were allowed by the government to run their course.

As a vehicle for constitutional reform and change — the hope of the moderates in 1905 — the Duma was a failure. It could debate issues and make recommendations, but it could not alone introduce measures into law. Furthermore, the tsar could dissolve it if he wished. The Duma had no control over government ministers; they remained answerable only to the tsar. The Duma was a toothless organisation in which the liberal opposition could play itself out with little real prospect of having any impact on tsarist rule. Without a free public sphere of politics in which political parties could act independently and issues could be raised and vigorously discussed, an assembly like the Duma was bound to encourage disillusionment among the politically aware sections of Russian society.

Marxism first entered Russia in the 1880s. It was seen by many in the intelligentsia as a way out of the dead end the revolutionary movement had drifted into after the assassination of Alexander II in 1881. Marxist study circles had developed in the 1880s and 1890s, and repression by the tsarist authorities forced many of those who were to become most prominent in the Marxist movement, including Vladimir Lenin, Georgii Plekhanov and Iulii Martov, to emigrate to Western Europe. In the early years of this century, the main concentrations of Russian Marxists lived in the large cities of the West.

An attempt was made in 1898 to launch a Russian Marxist party, the Russian Social Democratic Labour Party, but it bore little immediate fruit. The delegates to the Foundation Congress were arrested, with the result that the party existed in nothing but name until the so-called Second Congress was convened in 1903. But at this time of its organisational birth, the party experienced the split that was to be of fundamental importance to the future of Russian Marxism. This split, formally over the definition of a party member, saw the emergence of the Bolsheviks and the Mensheviks.

Bolshevism and Menshevism

In 1902 Lenin published his famous pamphlet *What is to be Done?* in which he outlined his view of how, under current conditions, a revolutionary party should be structured. Lenin argued that, by itself, the working class was unable to achieve the class consciousness that would enable it to understand its real

St Petersburg, 1897: Leaders of the League of Struggle for the Emancipation of the Working Class, one of the first Marxist groups in Russia. Lenin is seated in the centre, Martov is seated on the right (Hulton Deutsch)

interests. He believed that the real interests of the working class lay in the overthrow of the existing system and its replacement by socialism. By itself, the working class was able to attain only trade union consciousness, the false view that its best interests were served through the struggle for partial improvements in working conditions. True class consciousness could be brought to the workers only from outside, by revolutionary intellectuals. It was this sort of person who should lead the political organisation of the working class, the revolutionary party. But under current conditions of tsarist oppression, Lenin argued, the party could not afford to be a broad structure freely open to all members of the working class. The only way it could survive was if it was a party of professional revolutionaries, characterised by centralism, discipline and tight unity. One implication of this view was that while workers could become party members, they could do so only by becoming professional revolutionaries and thereby in part transcending their class origins. This also meant that they would become in some sense classless, losing touch with those fellow members of their class who remained working on the factory floor.

Over the years there has been a good deal of confusion about the position Lenin set forth in this pamphlet. Some have suggested that Lenin's outline for a party in *What is to be Done?* was the desired model for a workers' party under all circumstances, including when the Bolsheviks were in power. The pamphlet, however, was written with specific reference to the problems faced by the workers' movement in turn-of-the-century Russia. This period was, in terms of the Marxist outlook adopted by Lenin, the final phase of the feudal period of development. Russian Marxists accepted the scheme of historical development presented by Marx, which saw society passing through distinct stages: slavery, feudalism, capitalism and finally communism. Lenin believed that the coming revolution in Russia would be the bourgeois-democratic revolution, which would bring into existence a bourgeois capitalist system. This would in turn create the conditions for socialist revolution. The type of party Lenin sketched in his pamphlet was directly related to the conditions, and the level of working-class consciousness, immediately prior to the bourgeois democratic revolution. There was no necessary link between this situation and type of party and the type of party that would be appropriate on the eve of the socialist revolution. *What is to be Done?* did not provide a universally applicable blueprint.

Lenin's view of the nature of the party in 1902 was reflected in his definition of a party member in 1903. The draft definitions suggested by Lenin and the future Menshevik leader Martov were as follows:

> 66 Lenin: A Party member is one who accepts the Party's program and supports the Party both financially and by personal participation in one of its organisations. 99

> 66 Martov: A member of the Russian Social-Democratic Labour Party is one who, accepting its program, works actively to accomplish its aims under the control and direction of the organs of the Party. 99

PROBLEMS AND ISSUES
● Role of the party

PROBLEMS AND ISSUES
● Ideology — in theory

'Draft Rules of the RSDLP', V.I. Lenin, *Collected Works*, Vol.6, Moscow, 1964, p.476

'One Step Forward, Two Steps Back', Lenin, *Collected Works*, Vol.7, p.246

The difference between these formulations lay in Lenin's insistence on members participating in a party organisation compared with Martov's view that working under the direction of such an organisation was sufficient. Lenin's definition implied a tighter organisational structure while Martov's allowed for, in the term used at the time, a certain 'elasticity'. There were two views of the party implicit here, with Martov's involving greater openness to the working class (and in Lenin's view to the tsarist police) than did Lenin's. This issue, combined with some important differences over questions of revolutionary theory and a dispute about membership of the editorial board of the party newspaper *Iskra*, led to a split. Those who followed Lenin were called the Bolsheviks (majority) and those who followed Martov the Mensheviks (minority). Despite a paper reconciliation in 1906, these groups remained largely separate thereafter. Russian social democracy was considerably weakened by the continual manoeuvring and conflict between these two groups.

From the time of their emergence in 1903 until 1917, the Bolsheviks were a minor political force in Russia. Like most other revolutionary groups, the Bolshevik Party consisted of two distinct parts. Most of its members lived and worked in Russia, in the underground. In many parts of the country Bolshevik committees and cells existed, attempting to radicalise the working class and to extend their base of support in working-class society. The party played only a minor role in the 1905 Revolution. Its more important task was the consolidation of its position in Russia. By 1917, despite continuing arrests of activists by the tsarist police, the party had developed a network of party cells in the industrial areas of the country.

There was a big gap between the undergrounders, typified by future leaders Stalin and Molotov, and the other part of the party gathered around Lenin in emigration. The group living in exile in the West was fractious, argumentative and forever involved in disputes about points of theoretical and organisational detail. The most important of those in exile was Lenin. Always confident of the correctness of his own views, Lenin continually engaged in disputes with those around him who, in his view, supported wrong policy positions. Although Lenin was the most prominent of the Bolsheviks, he was far from being their unchallenged leader. He always had to fight to get his views accepted and, although he usually got his way, his colleagues often retained serious doubts about the correctness of his views. Lenin's authority was by no means absolute among either his fellow exiles or the undergrounders at work in Russia. For much of the time, the latter followed their own policy lines independent of Lenin and his colleagues.

POPULAR UNREST AND THE WAR

PROBLEMS
AND ISSUES
● Modernisation

Following the suppression of the 1905 Revolution, levels of popular unrest declined significantly. As the war approached, however, social tensions again began to build. These were caused by the government's failure to meet the problems posed by rapid industrialisation. There had been little improvement in the lot of the urban workers. Both living and working conditions remained bad and, despite the legalisation of trade unions in 1905, there was little organisational protection for workers against management. Strikes remained illegal. In the countryside, peasant land hunger remained unsatisfied. Peasant resentment was strengthened by the effects of the Stolypin reforms and by the state pressure on the peasants to maintain agricultural deliveries in order to expand industrial production. In 1912, strike activity jumped enormously, as the following figures (which probably understate the actual number) show. The figures relate to the empire as a whole.

Table 1.4   Strike Activity 1905–14

	Total strikes	Political strikes
1905	13 995	6024
1906	6114	2950
1907	3573	2558
1908	892	464
1909	340	50
1910	222	8
1911	466	24
1912	2032	1300
1913	2404	1034
1914 (Jan–July)	3534	2401

Leopold Haimson, 'The Problem of Social Stability in Urban Russia, 1905–1917', *Slavic Review*, 23(4), 1964, p.627

It is clear that the official response to the 1905 Revolution had not dealt with the underlying causes of the Revolution or the fundamental complaints of the populace. Labour unrest was becoming so bad that some observers believed the tsar could not risk mobilising his army for war in August 1914.

- Draw a graph of strike activity as depicted in Table 1.4.
- How did the proportion of political strikes change?

Responses to War

The outbreak of the war led to a surge of patriotism in Russia as elsewhere, and a dramatic decline in popular unrest. The populace rallied behind the government in support of the war effort, creating a mood that was hostile to any anti-war sentiment. Most Russian political groups adopted either an openly patriotic stand or took up a defensist position. Defensism involved support for the war effort to defend Russian territory, but no support once that war became offensive and aggressive. Lenin and the Bolsheviks took neither of these positions. Lenin believed that the war was an imperialist war and that defeat for Russia could lead to civil war and revolution. Lenin therefore

PROBLEMS AND ISSUES

- Role of the party

The outbreak of war led to mass mobilisation in Russia (UPI/ Bettmann)

The war caused great hardship for the urban population of Russia, and food and fuel were in short supply. Pictured is a milk queue in Moscow (UPI/ Bettmann)

adopted a defeatist position. This was very unpopular, both among other revolutionary groups and the population at large; soon after the war began all known Bolsheviks in Russia were arrested. The Bolsheviks gained support as labour unrest grew, however, particularly when popular support for the war began to evaporate in 1916. This made their anti-war position less objectionable.

The surge of patriotic enthusiasm for the war soon waned. Initially peasant agriculture was stimulated by the war, but the war brought ill effects for the peasantry the longer it dragged on. Shortages of labour began to occur as men and horses were mobilised for the front. Increasingly, goods that the peasants needed to buy both for everyday life and to repair agricultural equipment could not be obtained. In the cities, the workers were subjected to increased demands as industry sought to sustain the war effort. Longer hours, harsher conditions and wartime shortages stimulated worker discontent.

The increased pressures on these two sections of the population may not have mattered if the war had gone well. But soon after its outbreak, the Russian forces were in difficulties. In the first months of the war, shortages of supplies left many parts of the army without sufficient weapons and ammunition, and without proper clothing to guard against the onset of winter. A series of heavy defeats on the battlefield led to widespread disillusionment in Russia, which soon developed into a major crisis for the tsarist system. In mid-1915 Nicholas had taken up the position of commander-in-chief of the Russian forces. He was now directly responsible for the army's performance. But Nicholas seems to have had few military skills and was surrounded by officers with similar limitations. The Stavka (General Headquarters) headed by the tsar projected an image of incompetence.

A similar image existed in the sphere of civilian government, where personal favouritism in the selection of ministers allowed many inexperienced and incompetent people to hold office. What added to the public dismay at this situation was that with the tsar away at the Stavka for long periods of time, his wife Tsarina Alexandra played a prominent role in governmental affairs. Her German birth gave rise to many rumours about her loyalty laying with Germany rather than Russia. The effect of this was strengthened by the influence that Rasputin was able to exercise over her. Believed by the tsarina to be a man of God who could help her haemophiliac son, Rasputin wielded significant influence in the court. He was widely seen as a malevolent influence. With Nicholas away, rumours of scandals were rife. Despite the murder of Rasputin late in 1916, the image of the tsar and of tsarist rule as backward, incompetent and dominated by religious mysticism became firmly implanted in many sections of the community.

During the reign of Nicholas II, Russian society moved to the watershed of 1917. The forces leading to revolution were powerful, but they were not inevitable. Ultimately, the principal force propelling society toward revolution was the rapid industrialisation on which the state had embarked. Inevitably this process produced strains within society, particularly among those who had to pay for industrial growth, the peasants and workers. But the government and the tsar were out of tune with popular sentiment. Few steps were taken

PROBLEMS AND ISSUES
- Modernisation
- Revolution

Much of Russian society was scandalised by the relationship that was believed to exist between Rasputin and the royal family. In this caricature, the tsar and tsarina are shown as puppets of Rasputin (Hoover Institution Archives, California)

Review and discuss

- As a patriotic middle-class Russian citizen, write one paragraph on your reaction to this poster.
- What form did modernisation take in Russia in the late nineteenth and early twentieth centuries? What problems did it produce? How serious were they? How did the tsar respond? Why?
- Discuss in class why so much change results from involvement in war.

to meet the demands coming from below, with the result that disillusionment was bound to develop. Badly advised and obsessed with the desire to pass the throne on to his heir with no reduction in its powers, the tsar was unwilling to give the different social groups in Russian society a meaningful part to play in the political process. He refused to use the Duma as a means of co-opting important social groups into the governing structure. Shortsighted and obsessed with the tradition of the unlimited tsar, Nicholas was unable to promote the sorts of changes within the political structure which would have made it more relevant. Instead, the political system remained little changed in essentials while the society was undergoing a social and economic revolution brought on by industrialisation. The war merely sharpened these contradictions and hastened the revolution.

The Fall of the Tsarist Autocracy

When Tsar Nicholas II abdicated from the throne in favour of his brother Grand Duke Mikhail on 2 March 1917, who in turn renounced the throne on 3 March, the Russian monarchy came to an end. Why did it fall so suddenly? How could a monarchy that had lasted so long topple so swiftly? This case study will survey some of the explanations given for this. Publications mentioned are listed at the end. Among the most commonly offered explanations, the following four have been prominent:

- The monarchy was the victim of a conspiracy mounted by a small revolutionary group.
- The monarchy's ability to survive was fundamentally weakened by the nature of the leadership given by the tsar.
- The war placed such significant strains upon Russian society that the political structure could not withstand it.
- The position of the traditional tsarist autocracy was eroded by the social, economic and political changes brought about by industrialisation.

The first explanation is a *conspiracy theory*, the second a *personalist explanation*, the third a chance or *contingency explanation* (it was the chance occurrence of the war which brought the monarchy undone), and the fourth a *structural explanation*. No scholar accepts any of these as the sole explanation, but what is important is the weight given to each in the overall explanation of the February Revolution. What are each of these explanations?

Conspiracy Theory

An early version of this theory was offered by the Bolshevik Alexander Shliapnikov who argued that Bolsheviks in Russia were expecting revolution in the period leading up to 23 February 1917, and when it broke out were able to take over its leadership. This is despite being isolated from the more prominent leaders of the party like Lenin. A more forthright assertion of this type of argument is to be found in the infamous Stalinist *Short Course* history of the Party (see p.177) which declared 'the Bolsheviks were directly leading the struggle of the masses in the streets…'

One variant on this type of approach is offered by George Katkov who argues that a major role was played in bringing about the revolution by agents and conspirators working on behalf of, or at least financed by, the Germans.

PROBLEMS
AND ISSUES
- Revolution
- Role of the party

Tsarist Leadership

Most observers agree that Nicholas was not well-suited psychologically to the role he was called on to play. In personal matters he appears to have been kind and considerate of those around him and to have considerable patience. In political affairs, however, he was characterised by both obstinacy and indecisiveness. He was insistent throughout the crises of 1905 and the war that he would not give up any of the autocratic powers of the throne. He believed that it was his sacred duty to pass these on intact to his son. This meant that any concessions that were wrung from him, as in 1905, were both reluctantly given and withdrawn whenever possible. His indecisiveness, especially on major questions, left him open to reliance on advice which was not always well-founded.

This was particularly evident in the war when he seems to have been heavily influenced by his wife the tsarina, Alexandra, and the mystical holy man Rasputin. Rasputin's influence stemmed from his apparent ability to control the haemophilia of the heir to the throne, Alexei. When Nicholas took over personal command of the army, control over the government was effectively left in the hands of Alexandra and Rasputin. This scandalised reputable society, and the tsarina's German ancestry gave fuel to popular suspicions that the court was traitorous to the Russian cause. If it was not traitorous, in the view of important elements of society, it was incompetent. Even after the death of Rasputin in December 1916, the court clique dominated by Alexandra continued to exercise overwhelming influence over Nicholas. This clique reinforced him in his refusal to reshape the government and to replace many of the incompetent, conservative ministers he had appointed.

PROBLEMS AND ISSUES

● Revolution

Influenced by the conservative court clique and reinforced in his belief that his duty was not to weaken the autocrat's power, Nicholas blundered on. The government became even more out of touch with the war and the effects it was having than it already was. Bernard Pares emphasises the role and shortcomings of the court and tsar in leading to the fall of the monarchy.

The Role of the War

This explanation assumes that the war played a decisive role in the fall of the regime. In the words of one student 'many factors were responsible for the collapse of the autocratic system, the most important of course being the setbacks suffered in the war... The war catalysed the process of internal rot, leaving the ancient state unable to support the extra burdens placed upon it' (Geyer, p.54). This sort of explanation recognises that although all was not healthy with the tsarist regime, its collapse came about because of the extra pressures imposed by the war. Some supporters of this view believe that without the war, the tsarist system would have been able to ride out the longer term difficulties it faced. (For one scholar who changed his view on this question, see Kennan).

What were the effects of the war that are seen to have been so disastrous for the regime's survival? The Russian army sustained enormous losses, with some eight million soldiers dead, wounded, missing or prisoners of war. Each month about 350 000 soldiers recently inducted into the army, poorly trained and equipped, were sent to the front. There were continuing shortages of military supplies, and the financial problems of the government combined with disrupted transportation networks to ensure continuing problems at the front.

The problems at the front were matched by problems in the rear. By 1916 the strains of the war were telling. Food shortages and rising prices created severe difficulties for the population in both city and countryside. The strains placed on the economy to achieve increased production for the war effort were translated into heightened pressure in the workplace as employers sought to gain even more from their workers. Working conditions deteriorated and the army's continuing demand for new recruits robbed the factories and farms of much of their able-bodied workforce. As success continued to elude the army, demoralisation and discontent became widespread. From 1915 to 1916 the number of strikes doubled.

The war effort also heightened tensions between the monarchy and those sections of middle-class society that had become politically active through the Duma. The liberals, represented by the Kadet party and its leader Pavel Miliukov, argued that they should not share the burdens of war without at the same time being given some part in the direction of that war. In other words, that group in society which had sought to use the 1905 Revolution to wring political concessions from the tsar sought to use the war for the same purpose. But Nicholas's government did not accept the demands of liberal society and continued to try to exclude it from any meaningful part in political decision-making. This created great hostility between government and Duma and deprived the tsar of the support of the politically active middle class.

The war thus created significant tensions in Russian society; it sowed discontent in the army, disillusionment among workers and peasants, and disaffection within the middle class.

Structural Causes

PROBLEMS AND ISSUES
- Modernisation
- Revolution

The main thrust of this explanation is that the process of rapid industrialisation undertaken by the tsar so disrupted the traditional patterns of Russian society that the basis of the political structure was undermined. (For example, the work of Von Laue.) Industrialisation created a new urban working class which was herded into the cities, living and working under very difficult conditions, and with little opportunity to improve those conditions. The peasants left on the farms were taxed heavily to finance industrial development, which added to their long-standing grievances relating to land distribution. A middle class, including significant entrepreneurial elements, was emerging in the cities and seeking to expand its political influence to better foster and protect its interests. And finally, the traditional landowning nobility was being pushed increasingly to the side; their economic power was declining as industrial development became more important, and they were increasingly being ignored by the tsarist government.

This situation of rising new and declining old classes created a crisis for the regime. It was unwilling to respond satisfactorily to the demands of the workers, peasants and middle class, and could not rely on the declining nobility. As a result, the social basis of the regime became very narrow, resting overwhelmingly upon the bureaucracy. With increasing pressure from below and the regime's inability to react effectively to it, the further industrial development proceeded, the greater the alienation between state and society would become. This means that, even without the war, the pressures unleashed by industrial development would have engulfed the tsarist regime.

Which Explanation?

Which of these explanations is most satisfactory in explaining the fall of the tsarist regime? Is any one of them satisfactory? Or must they be used in combination?

The first explanation, the conspiracy theory, should be rejected as having any real explanatory value. The argument that the Bolsheviks led the February Revolution is a gross exaggeration. This argument originated in debates inside the Communist Party in the 1920s; the main aim of these debates was not historical accuracy but conflict over policy direction (Longley). It was then taken up during the Stalinist period as a means of boosting the historical importance of the Bolsheviks. In fact, the Bolsheviks played no effective leadership role at all in the February Revolution.

The Revolution began with a lockout at the Putilev works in Petrograd on 22 February. It was followed by a strike on the following day, which soon spread so that the strike became general. The tsar, still at the front, refused to accept the advice of the Duma that a new government headed by someone who was popularly trusted should be formed. Instead he ordered the troops to put down the strike and the rioting occurring throughout the city. After initially following orders, on 27 February the troops stationed in Petrograd began to mutiny and join the strikers; by 1 March, the whole Petrograd garrison had deserted the tsar and his government. The tsarist government, the Council of Ministers, ceased meeting while the Duma was closed by the tsar on 27 February. An informal group from the Duma continued to meet illegally and a week later formed the Provisional Government. On 27 February the Petrograd Soviet of Workers' and Soldiers' Deputies was summoned by worker representatives and left-wing intellectuals. It began to function as an alternative government. The tsar now sought to return to Petrograd. But he was advised by army chief of staff General Alekseyev that the army could not put down the rising and that the only course if the army was to stay in the field against the Germans was for the tsar to abdicate. On 2 March Nicholas abdicated.

No organised group led the Revolution. Despite some equivocation, the leading study of the February Revolution declares 'it is difficult to subscribe to the theory of Bolshevik leadership. The Bolshevik Party as a whole failed to react to the workers' strike movement quickly and imaginatively. The Russian Bureau led by Shliapnikov was constantly behind the developing events and grossly underestimated the revolutionary potentialities of the movement...' (Hasegawa). Nor is there any solid evidence of any groups working for the Germans having a significant impact on the course of events (see Katkov in Pipes).

PROBLEMS AND ISSUES
- Role of the party
- Modernisation

The most satisfactory explanation of the fall of the regime involves a combination of the other three explanations. The structural strains imposed on Russian society by industrialisation were significant, as the increasing levels of strike activity leading up to the war demonstrate. The effect of such strains was greatly increased by the war and the hardship it created. In the face of these continuing strains, the tsarist government could have sought agreement with emerging middle-class forces and thereby stabilised its political base. That it did not is due in large part to the refusal by the tsar, supported by his conservative advisers, to consider any erosion of his autocratic powers and prerogatives. His refusal to listen to more moderate advice and to seek to bring about a closer relationship between his government and society left it vulnerable when the strains within the society led to the eruption of February 1917.

This sort of explanation includes a variety of factors and, because of that, is much more satisfactory as a means of understanding the fall of the regime than any single factor explanation can possibly be.

List of references

Geyer, Dietrich, *The Russian Revolution. Historical Problems and Perspectives*, trans. Bruce Little, Berg Publishers, Leamington Spa, 1987.

Hasegawa, Tsuyoshi, *The February Revolution: Petrograd 1917*, University of Washington Press, Seattle and London, 1981.

History of the Communist Party of the Soviet Union (Bolsheviks), Short Course, Moscow, 1939.

Katkov, George, *Russia 1917. The February Revolution*, Longmans, London, 1967.

Katkov, George, 'German Political Intervention in Russia during World War I', and comments by Alexander Dallin, in Richard Pipes (ed.), *Revolutionary Russia: A Symposium*, Anchor Books, New York, 1969.

Kennan, George, 'The Breakdown of the Tsarist Autocracy', in Pipes, *Revolutionary Russia*.

Longley, D.A., 'Iakovlev's question, or the historiography of the problem of spontaneity and leadership in the Russian revolution of February 1917', in Edith Rogovin Frankel, Jonathan Frankel and Baruch Knei-paz (eds), *Revolution in Russia. Reassessments of 1917*, Cambridge University Press, Cambridge, 1992.

Pares, Sir Bernard, *The Fall of the Russian Monarchy*, Alfred A. Knopf, New York, 1939.

Shliapnikov, Alexander, *Semnadtsatyi god*, 4 vols, Moscow, 1923–31.

Von Laue, Theodore H., *Why Lenin? Why Stalin? A Reappraisal of the Russian Revolution, 1900–1930*, J.B. Lippincott Co, Philadelphia and New York, 1964.

Essay Questions

1 'The profound cause of the February 1917 Revolution was the failure of the tsarist system to cope with the disruption resulting from modernisation.' How valid is this assessment?

2 'World War I's enormously disruptive impact upon the Home Front goes a long way to explaining why Russia experienced revolution.' How satisfactory is this explanation of what occurred in Russia in February 1917?

3 How crucial were the actions of the Russian Army — initially in the form of the mutiny of the Petrograd garrison and finally in the pressure exerted by the High Command — in producing the collapse of the tsarist regime?

4 Was the February Revolution the unplanned result of the spontaneous actions of discontented soldiers and workers, or the product of careful planning by groups such as the Bolsheviks?

THE REVOLUTIONARY YEAR

CHAPTER TWO

1917

N 1917 the Russian monarchy fell, ending the 300-year-old Romanov dynasty. Its moderate successor lasted a mere eight months before giving way to the most radical of the organised political parties in Russia at that time. But that party, the Bolsheviks, had been a very minor group at the time of the tsar's fall. Within eight months it had gone from obscurity to power in the largest country on earth.

Focus questions

In order to understand the process whereby the Bolsheviks came to power, the following questions may be helpful:
- What was dual power?
- Why did the Provisional Government lose its authority in 1917?
- What role did mass unrest play in Bolshevik success?
- How important was Marxist theory to ultimate Bolshevik success?

PROBLEMS AND ISSUES
- Revolution

The circumstances of the February Revolution (see Case Study 1), with spontaneous action from below toppling the tsar, made apparent the power and authority vacuum that existed in Russia. Two bodies emerged in the capital Petrograd* to fill this vacuum. One had its roots in the working class: the Soviet of Workers' Deputies. The other significant body was the Provisional Government, which had its roots in middle-class and professional Russia. The interaction of these two bodies was important for the course of the revolution.

* St Petersburg was the capital of Russia until 1914, when the name was changed to Petrograd. In 1924 Petrograd became Leningrad. In 1917 the capital was moved back to the ancient capital, Moscow.

The notorious Litovsky prison in Petrograd was assaulted and burned on 27 February 1917 (UPI/Bettmann)

THE SOVIET OF WORKERS' AND SOLDIERS' DEPUTIES

The Soviet of Workers' Deputies was formed on 27 February; from 1 March it was called the Soviet of Workers' and Soldiers' Deputies. This organisation was based on the experience of 1905 and, at least in its plenary or general assembly, was manned by representatives of Petrograd factory workers and the troops. The Soviet consisted of an executive committee, which was elected by the plenary assembly, and the assembly itself. In the latter, a principle of recall operated whereby individual factories or soldiers' companies could replace their delegates whenever they wished. This meant there was some fluidity in the membership of the Soviet, and it provided a channel through which changing popular opinion could be reflected in the meetings of the Soviet. Most delegates were ordinary factory workers and soldiers. In contrast, the executive committee was dominated by moderate socialist intellectuals. These people were more at home in the field of socialist theory than the ordinary rank-and-file delegates. Importantly they were also much less sensitive to the dramatic changes in mood that were to occur at the lower levels of Russian society in the following months. This was to have significant implications for the future of Russia.

The Soviet found itself at the head of the working people. In the words of its 28 February appeal to the people:

> In order to succeed in this struggle for democracy, the people must create their own governmental organ. Yesterday, February 27, there was formed at the capital a Soviet of Workers' Deputies, made up of representatives of factories, mills, mutinied troops, and democratic and socialistic parties and groups. The Soviet, sitting in the Duma, has set for itself as its main task the organisation of the popular forces, and the fight for the consolidation

'To the People of Petrograd and Russia from the Soviet of Workers' Deputies', Robert Paul Browder and Alexander F. Kerensky (eds). *The Russian Provisional Government 1917 Documents*, Stanford University Press, Stanford, 1961, p.78

of political freedom and popular government... All together, with our forces united, we will fight to wipe out completely the old Government and to call a constituent assembly on the basis of universal, equal, direct, and secret suffrage.

"

While repeating the long-held socialist call for a Constituent Assembly to determine the ultimate fate of Russia, the Soviet was nevertheless the most authoritative contemporary organ in the eyes of the Petrograd populace. Popular allegiance effectively made it the most powerful body in the capital: the general strike ended only when the Soviet called on the workers to return to work, newspapers were published after a decision by the Soviet, and it was this body which negotiated an eight-hour working day with employers. But this power did not, and in a revolutionary situation could not, rest on notions of formal or constitutional authority. The authority the Soviet enjoyed stemmed purely from popular support.

THE PROVISIONAL GOVERNMENT

The second body to emerge at this time was the Provisional Government. This was formed on 2 March by an informal temporary committee of the State Duma, a body that had no standing even in tsarist constitutional law. The Provisional Government was formed neither from below nor by anyone with a popular mandate. The State Duma had been elected on a strictly limited franchise, while the Provisional Government itself was never subjected to the testing of the ballot box. Democratic it was not. It was the product of middle-

The Duma meeting in late February 1917. Days later the Tsar Nicholas II, shown in the portrait which towers over the proceedings, was overthrown (UPI/ Bettmann)

class and professional Russia and was dominated by members of right-wing parties like the Constitutional Democrats (Kadets) and the Octobrists and by formally unaffiliated conservatives, like the first prime minister Prince Lvov. The only member on the left of the political spectrum in the first Provisional Government, which ruled from March to the beginning of May, was justice minister and Socialist Revolutionary Alexander Kerensky. Overwhelmingly liberal and conservative in its make-up, the tenor and political complexion of the Provisional Government were clearly at odds with those of the Soviet.

Dual Power

From the outset, the Provisional Government was in an anomalous position. It had neither an electoral base nor a legislative assembly to sustain it. Instead it rested on the bureaucracy inherited from the tsar, the support of organisations like the War Industries Committee and the army High Command, and the international recognition quickly offered by Russia's wartime allies. In the face of the popularly-based Soviet, the Provisional Government seemed particularly isolated in Russian society.

The relationship between Soviet and Provisional Government has been called *dual power*, a situation in which two bodies claiming national jurisdiction knocked uneasily against one another in the vacuum created by the tsar's fall. Neither had clearly defined powers or rights, and the relationship between them was unclear. The potential for conflict seemed high, but in practice there was little disagreement between them for most of the February–October period. Relations were most harmonious following the creation of the first coalition government in May, discussed below.

One way in which the Provisional Government could have bolstered its position was by building its support among the population at large. But this it failed to do.

POPULAR EXPECTATIONS

PROBLEMS AND ISSUES
● Revolution

The fall of the tsar unleashed a torrent of popular expectations and a surge of enthusiasm for the new government. But this enthusiasm rested on the assumption that the government would act to satisfy those expectations. What sorts of expectations were raised?

The Peasants

Peasant aspirations were reflected in the resolutions of peasant meetings and in the messages and demands sent to the government. Some of these embraced political issues like the need for a democratic republic and for action against the tsar and the upper classes, but for the most part they concentrated on issues much closer to home.

The areas of most concern were land, food supply and local administration. **Land:** The tsar's fall was widely interpreted as symbolising the end of the unjust landholding system in the country. Peasants believed that:

L.S. Gaponenko (ed.), *Revoliutsionnoe dvizhenie v Rossii v aprele 1917g. Aprel'skii krizis: Dokumenty i materialy,* Moscow, 1958, p.610

> 66 land, as a blessing created by nature, can be used by all who wish to work it with their own personal strength, without hired labour, but no more than the labour norm. 99

In most parts of the country, this demand effectively constituted a call for the destruction of non-peasant landholding in the countryside. In particular it meant the passing of all noble land into peasant hands.

Food supply: The peasant demand on this question was that the grain market be regulated in a way that would encourage farmers to produce and sell large quantities of grain to satisfy the needs of consumers.

Local administration: The collapse of the old order was interpreted in the villages as the end of the unjust system of authority relations in the countryside, whereby the peasants were ruled by non-peasant landowners or by officials sent by Petrograd. In the words of one peasant delegate to the Moscow Soviet on 6 March:

Gaponenko, *Revoliutsionnoe dvizhenie,* p.670

> 66 it is necessary to hold new elections for all rural and village officials, to cleanse the country of remnants of the old regime, to remove land captains, police and others. 99

The peasants wanted to run their own lives without outside interference.

The Working Class

Like the peasantry, urban workers also made political demands, but once again most concern was expressed about those issues, usually economic, of immediate relevance to their lives. Of principal interest were working conditions: the eight-hour day, wage increases and security of employment were common matters of concern. The approach to these issues reflected distrust of the existing factory management, but initially this was not translated into a demand for a form of workers' control to replace existing factory authorities with people from the shop floor. When workers' control was mentioned early in the year, it usually meant checking and supervising the actions of management rather than replacing that management. It was thus related much more to concerns about living standards and working conditions than to socialist theory. For the workers, then, the fall of the tsar was seen as a signal for the improvement of their living and working conditions.

Soldiers

Initially there was surprisingly little overt anti-war sentiment, even among the soldiers. The tsar's fall produced a surge of patriotism, reflected in a short-term increased flow of grain to the authorities. Among the soldiers, outright opposition to the war was, at least at first, usually muted. While the desire for peace was strongly reflected in the soldiers' demands, this did not necessarily imply an immediate downing of weapons. Soldiers wanted the new government to work towards peace with the Germans. More immediately, they wanted traditional authority relationships within the army reworked, an aim achieved by the famous Order Number One of the Petrograd Soviet. This allowed the soldiers to elect their own committees and made the troops subordinate to the Soviet, thereby destroying the authority of their officers. In addition, the soldiers were concerned about the welfare of their families at home, and since most soldiers came from the villages, many of their demands echoed those of the peasants.

National Minorities

The national minorities in what had been the Russian empire had long been restive under Russian rule. The tsar's fall was interpreted as meaning the opening of the doors of the so-called 'prison house of peoples'. Educated elites in the non-Russian areas hoped that the new order in Russia would mean, if not national independence, at least greater autonomy. Other segments of the non-Russian population also voiced such sentiments, along with the same sorts of concerns that moved the peasants and workers of Russia.

THE GOVERNMENT'S RESPONSE

These aspirations constituted the standards by which the people could judge the Provisional Government. If the government was able to satisfy those aspirations, it would gain popular support and consolidate its authority among the masses. If it failed to satisfy popular aspirations, its isolation would be increased and its lack of support laid bare for all to see. The initial surge of support for the Provisional Government would quickly evaporate unless some progress in satisfying those expectations was made. Unfortunately little such progress was made.

A foretaste of the government's failure is to be found in the list of guiding principles issued at the time of its formation:

> 1. An immediate and complete amnesty in all cases of a political and religious nature, including terrorist acts, military revolts and agrarian offenses etc.
>
> 2. Freedom of speech, press, and assembly, and the right to unionise and strike with the extension of political freedom to persons serving in the armed forces as limited by the exigencies of military and technical circumstances.
>
> 3. The abolition of all restrictions based on class, religion, and nationality.
>
> 4. The immediate preparation for the convocation of the Constituent Assembly on the basis of universal, equal, direct suffrage and secret ballot, which will determine the form of government and the constitution of the country.
>
> 5. The substitution of a people's militia for the police, with elective officers responsible to the organs of local self-government.
>
> 6. Elections to the organs of local self-government are to be held on the basis of universal, direct, equal suffrage and secret ballot.
>
> 7. Those military units which took part in the revolutionary movement shall be neither disarmed nor withdrawn from Petrograd.
>
> 8. While preserving strict military discipline on duty and during military service, the soldiers are to be freed from all restrictions in the exercise of those civil rights to which all other citizens are entitled.
>
> The Provisional Government considers it its duty to add that it had not the slightest intention of taking advantage of the military situation to delay in any way the realisation of reforms and the measures outlined above.

'From the Provisional Government', Browder & Kerensky, *Russian Provisional Government*, p.135

Review

- Considering the demands of the peasantry, the workers, the soldiers and the national minorities, do these principles seem likely to satisfy expectations?
- What important concerns of the main sectors of the population are not addressed in this document?
- Compare this document with what you know about Order Number One of the Petrograd Soviet. What differences do you see?

Peasant Concerns

On the land question, the government adopted a policy of freezing land relations pending a final resolution by the Constituent Assembly. Special organs, the land committees, were established on 21 April at the national, provincial, county and parish levels to act as the main instruments of government policy in the countryside.

> [They were to] be responsible for the collection of information on local land arrangements and land needs of the population, and the resolution of disputes and misunderstandings on land matters during the transitional period up until the implementation of land reform by the Constituent Assembly.

Vestnik Vremennago Pravitel'stva 38, 23 April 1917

These bodies were thus meant to collect the information necessary for future land reform and to resolve any disputes that might arise in the interim. Meanwhile, the peasants were called upon to refrain from any land seizures and patiently await resolution of this whole question by the Constituent Assembly. From as early as the end of March, the government sought to use armed force to suppress rural disturbances. As the year wore on and peasant land seizures became more violent, the use of armed force came even more to the fore.

The government sought to come to grips with the food supply question by imposing a state monopoly on grain with fixed prices to be administered by food committees. The fixed price was set at a level 60 per cent above that set by the tsarist government in 1916. There were two main problems with this policy. Firstly, the comprehensive survey of grain, landholdings and the local economic situation necessary for the monopoly to operate effectively was never completed. This meant there was no accepted basis on which food committees could secure the grain; either the old imperial formula was adopted or grain was taken in amounts arbitrarily decided by the food committees themselves. In either event, without agreement on the quantities to be procured by the state, this was widely seen by the peasants as little short of robbery. Secondly, and more importantly, the monopoly provided no incentive for producers to surrender their grain. Although grain prices were pegged, the prices of consumer goods the peasants wished to buy were not. Grain producers were caught between fixed prices for their produce and rising prices for the goods they sought to purchase. This provided them with no incentive to sell their grain; even the doubling of the fixed grain price on 27 August had little impact. The government was thus unable to regularise the grain market to ensure an adequate supply of grain to all.

Formally the government's policy on local government rested on a general commitment to the rule of law and administration by democratically elected bodies. But in practice its policy is summarised by the following statement:

L.S. Gaponenko et al (eds), *Revoliutsionnoe dvizhenie v Rossii posle sverzheniia samoderzhaviia: Dokumenty i materialy,* Moscow, 1957, p.422

> 66 ... it is desirable to retain, wherever possible, the entire existing administrative mechanism, with the aim of upholding the normal course of life in the country. 99

Local authorities were called upon to use local landowners (i.e. nobles) in an administrative capacity. This was bound to make local government organs appear alien to the peasants and, insofar as the latter's concerns focused upon the peasant acquisition of noble land, unsympathetic to peasant desires. This alienation was increased by local government organs being located in the towns rather than among the peasants themselves.

Workers' Demands

The government's approach to issues raised by the industrial working class was to attempt to hold the line against and to moderate the effect of the workers' demands. The government's declared aim was to establish proper relations between labour and capital based on 'law and justice'. To this end, conciliation chambers and factory committees, both of which were given legal

On 23 March 1917, a million people marched through Petrograd to pay tribute to the 184 people who died in the February Revolution (Russian Picture Collection, Hoover Institution Archives)

standing by government legislation, were established. The worker–management relationship in the factory was to be conducted through these bodies. But the powers given to the factory committees by the government were much narrower than those envisaged by the workers. They clearly reflected the main aim of the government, which was to maintain as much of the status quo in the factories as possible. The government supported management attempts to restore discipline in the factories, refused to enact legislation bringing in the eight-hour day, and failed to support any move in the direction of workers' control. This unwillingness to sanction significant changes to working conditions was matched by an inability to stop declining living standards in the cities and increasing unemployment. Both of these are linked with the failure to satisfy peasant grievances, and are discussed below.

Soldiers' Demands

The policy on the war remained an issue throughout the government's life. Its basic position was that Russia should stay in the war until the allies were victorious. Perhaps deluded by the initial surge of patriotism in February–March, caught by feelings of honour and obligation to the allies, and seduced by the promise of territorial gains on the war's successful conclusion, Foreign Affairs Minister Miliukov publicly campaigned for Russia to stay in the war until it was successfully completed. The Petrograd Soviet, and doubtless many in the trenches, believed that Russia should fight only a defensive war until a just peace 'with no annexations and indemnities' could be secured. Although

Public demonstrations were common in the capital between the revolutions. This is a pro-government demonstration. The banner reads: 'War for freedom to a victorious end' (Mrs G. Allen)

Miliukov was forced to resign in early May following public demonstrations opposing his policy (an act which led to the Soviet gaining a direct stake in the government through a coalition arrangement — see p.41), the government's policy remained basically unchanged. In June, War Minister Kerensky even launched a massive Russian offensive. Despite its failure, the government refused to even consider a separate peace with Germany to end the war.

National Minorities' Grievances

When confronted with calls for national independence, the government refused to acknowledge their legitimacy. Only in the case of Poland, which was behind German lines and therefore physically outside government control, did the government accept such demands and recognise Polish independence. All other nationalities were called upon to wait for the Constituent Assembly, which was the only body that could make these sorts of decisions.

Review

- Consider the responses of the Provisional Government to the demands of these various sectors in Russian society.

What section of Russian society did the Provisional Government seem to represent?

THE BASIS OF GOVERNMENT INACTION

Why didn't the government act decisively to satisfy the aspirations of these different sections of the population? Why on all major issues did it adopt a policy of seeking to avoid major change? One reason is that the members of the Provisional Government firmly believed that they were merely holding power in trust; that only the Constituent Assembly elected democratically by the Russian people had the right to make lasting changes to the social, economic and political structure of the country. Important too was the chronic lack of unity within the government. Split by party political divisions, widely differing political perspectives and intense personality conflicts, the government was unable to reach general agreement on the more pressing issues of the day, and those issues concerned the aspirations of the populace.

It is important to recognise that many of the demands being made on the government were impossible to meet in the conditions of revolutionary Russia. There was no way to overcome the traditional antagonisms between peasant and landowner, factory worker and manager, and rank-and-file soldier and officer. Nor was there any easy solution to the disruption to the market that was responsible for the food shortages. The government was surely correct in its belief that equitable solutions to these problems were impossible given the disruption Russia was experiencing. But in the short term such a position was politically naive and certain to cost the government dearly in terms of loss of authority and support. The government's position may have been defensible had it moved quickly to convene the Constituent Assembly. But it did not show any speed or decisiveness in taking the steps necessary to convene that body. Instead it procrastinated, pleading the obstacles created by revolutionary and war-time conditions. Such a stance proved disastrous.

Alexander Kerensky, prime minister of Russia from July 1917. He was forced to flee abroad when the Bolsheviks took power (Mrs G. Allen)

POPULAR RESPONSE TO GOVERNMENT POLICY

**PROBLEMS
AND ISSUES**
● Revolution

The government's stand accelerated the radicalisation of the popular mood, which was the single most important force for revolution and Bolshevik victory. In the countryside, this radicalisation was evident in the increased levels of disturbances. This is shown by the table below, which shows the monthly share of all unrest in the February–October period.

Graeme J. Gill, *Peasants and Government in the Russian Revolution*, London, Macmillan, 1979, p.189

Table 2.1   Peasant Unrest 1917

March	April	May	June	July	August	September	October
1.9	7.1	11.6	16.6	17.1	13.1	16.0	16.6

Levels of land seizure were high from April onwards, and became increasingly destructive and violent in the second half of the year. The established structure of land relations was destroyed as the lands and estates of private landowners were seized and passed into peasant hands. The peasants also seized control of crops, livestock and free-standing forest. The following despatch to the Ministry of the Interior gives a sense of what was happening in the countryside:

> 66 In the first days of October individual communities began to make demands to estate owners to transfer the estates [into] the direction of the communities and [in cases of] non-implemention of the demands they threatened *pogrom*. Up to this night there have been thefts of harvested grain and live and dead stock from the farms, and the felling of trees has taken on a general epidemic character. The estates of Tulinov, Vereshchagin, Levshin, Unkovskii, Kremlev and Trishatnii have been destroyed; grain, livestock and implements have been plundered, and information has been received about the destruction of other estates also in Efremov, Bogoroditsk and Venev counties. Trees have been felled within the bounds of every wooded area of the province, with the difference that in one place it is less, in another more. Trees are destroyed in the most rapacious way, not taking account of the age and worth of the trees. 99

D.A. Chugaev et al (eds), *Revoliutsionnoe dvizhenie v Rossii nakanune oktiabr'skogo vooruzhennogo vosstania 1–24 okt. 1917g. Dokumenty i materialy*, Moscow, 1962, p.447

The authority of urban-based local government organs was rejected as the peasants turned inward on their communities, obeying only their own organisations rooted in the villages. The official rural authority structure collapsed, and with it went the ability of any central government to exercise control over the rural areas. The city no longer ruled the countryside.

The most graphic demonstration of the loss of control by the city over the countryside was the peasants' reaction to the government's policy on the grain question. Rather than sell grain at prices they considered too low, peasant producers withheld it from the state. They preferred to hoard the grain, to distil it into alcohol, and even to destroy it rather than give it up to the government. The effect of this was compounded by a crop failure in the main

European grain-producing region, the Central Agricultural–Middle Volga area. The result was widespread food shortages in the grain-consuming north of the country and in the cities. This meant that the government could not ensure a continuing food supply to the urban areas.

Radicalisation in the Cities

In the cities, the radicalisation of the mood of the working class proceeded apace. As the year wore on, food shortages became more acute, unemployment increased, all sorts of goods became more difficult to obtain, and inflation meant effective cuts to workers' real wages. According to one study, market prices in Petrograd rose 34 times (i.e. goods were 34 times more expensive at the end of the year than at the beginning). By October real wage levels had fallen by between 10 per cent and 60 per cent of the January figure. Strike levels increased dramatically.

S.A. Smith, *Red Petrograd. Revolution in the Factories 1917–1918*, Cambridge University Press, Cambridge, 1983, p.116

Table 2.2 Number of Strikers (nationally)

April	June	September	October
35 000	175 000	1 100 000	1 200 000

The strikes became more organised and more radical in their demands, although they remained principally related to employment conditions rather than political questions. This is reflected in the following table:

Diane P. Koenker & William G. Rosenberg, 'Perceptions and Realities of Labour Protest, March to October 1917', in Edith Rogovin Frankel, Jonathan Frankel & Baruch Knei-Paz (eds), *Revolution in Russia. Reassessments of 1917*, Cambridge University Press, Cambridge, 1992, p.132

Table 2.3 Number of Strikers Involved in Strikes Over Different Types of Issues

Wages	1 800 000
Hours	1 250 000
Rules	400 000
Political issues	250 000

As the year wore on, factory seizures, strike activity and popular demonstrations reflected the radicalisation of working-class opinion.

The radicalisation of the workers also saw strengthening of such organisations as factory committees, trade unions and local soviets. Particularly important were the factory committees. They played a major role in asserting worker control in the factories, being involved in questions of the hiring and firing of labour, working conditions, and oversight and supervision of the general management and functioning of the factory. Acting in the name of the workers, factory committees, trade unions and soviets established effective control of the streets of the capital; the government ceased to have authority in the eyes of the working class. With the evaporation of governmental authority and increased working-class power, many factory owners lost control over their property. The roots of the established order had been cut.

Workers' organisations were also important as vehicles for promoting working-class consciousness. By organising workers to act collectively in pursuit of common aims, these bodies enhanced the sense of being part of a broader social grouping and of having interests separate from and perhaps in conflict with those of other groups. This sharpened workers' appreciation of the Bolsheviks as representative of their interests.

Soldiers

Armed soldiers demonstrating in Moscow, 1917 (Mary Evans/Alexander Medelin Collection)

At the front, many soldiers responded to the government's policies by deserting. They streamed back into the Russian countryside, injecting their own dose of radicalism into the already discontented villages. There are no satisfactory figures on desertion levels, but impressionistic evidence suggests that it was increasing markedly in the middle and latter parts of the year. Those who remained at the front hardly constituted a recognisable army. Order Number One of the Petrograd Soviet had undermined the position of the officers, with the result that there was little discipline in many parts of the army. As a fighting force, it had decayed from within.

National Minorities

Among the nationalities, the calls for independence became more strident. The Finnish parliament (the Sejm) vigorously asserted its right to independence, while the Ukrainian Central Rada moved during the year towards a rejection of Petrograd's authority. In areas as different as the Baltic regions and the Muslim areas of the Caucasus and Central Asia, pressures mounted to weaken the ties with the Russian centre.

THE POLITICS OF THE ELITE

It is within this context of the radicalisation of the popular mood that the actions of the elite political groups in the capital must be seen. The fall of the tsar had skewed the Russian political spectrum by moving it substantially to the left. The parties of the extreme right had virtually disappeared. As the popular mood became more radical, moving significantly to the left, the Provisional Government remained stranded on the right, without popular support. This discrediting of the Provisional Government also affected the moderate leadership of the Petrograd Soviet because of the organisational linkages established between these two bodies.

In the first Provisional Government this linkage had been informal, through the person of Kerensky who was a member of both bodies. In mid-April popular demonstrations broke out in the capital in opposition to the government's apparent policy of pursuing the war to a victorious conclusion. These demonstrations strengthened the position of the Soviet and weakened that of the government, which now collapsed. It was succeeded by a new coalition government that gave substantial representation to the socialist parties dominating the Soviet executive committee. Headed by the non-party Prince Lvov, this government had three Socialist Revolutionaries (SRs), three Mensheviks and one Popular Socialist, along with nine people from the moderate right. The second coalition government, which took office on 24 July and was headed by the SR Kerensky, had three SRs, three Mensheviks, two Popular Socialists and seven from the right. The third coalition, beginning on 25 September and also headed by Kerensky, had two SRs, four Mensheviks, four Kadets and seven non-party representatives.

The socialist parties and the Soviet executive committee were therefore well-represented in the government. Despite Kerensky's position as prime minister from July, however, there is no evidence that their presence made the government any more open to reform and change than it would otherwise have been. The most important effect of their involvement in the government was that they came to share the growing unpopularity of the government. For many, the participation of those parties in the government discredited both the parties themselves and the moderate leadership of the Soviet. But this discrediting of the parties did not extend to the Bolsheviks, who were not involved in the government.

Discuss

- If you were the leader of the Provisional Government, what policies would you have adopted in early 1917?

- What proposals would you have made to the third coalition government in September?

THE BOLSHEVIKS

Like everyone else, the Bolsheviks were surprised by the fall of the tsar. Lenin and the acknowledged leaders were in exile abroad, while the most important figures inside Russia were in prison or internal exile. With the release of political prisoners following the fall of the tsar, many of these returned to the capital. The leading party figures in Russia now became Joseph Stalin and Vyacheslav Molotov. It was mainly as a result of their efforts that the party adopted a policy of 'vigilant control' over the Provisional Government, support for the Petrograd Soviet, and pressure on the government to force it to seek peace negotiations with the Germans. These policies were based upon the ideological interpretation that the February Revolution was a bourgeois revolution, and that Russia was therefore destined to experience a prolonged period of bourgeois capitalist rule. This situation changed with Lenin's return to the capital, on a sealed train provided by the Germans, on 3 April.

Lenin's Intervention in April

Lenin's view on revolution in Russia had been changing during the war years. By widening his focus of analysis from Russia alone to global imperialism, he had arrived at a position virtually the same as that of 'permanent revolution' espoused by Leon Trotsky in 1905. In essentials, Lenin's view was that the weakness of the Russian bourgeoisie meant that it could not carry through the bourgeois revolution to its necessary conclusion. This could be done only by the proletariat which, by seizing power, could ensure that the bourgeois revolution was transformed into the socialist revolution. This would eliminate the need for a prolonged bourgeois phase of development and ensure that the society moved from the end of the feudal period to the beginnings of socialism in one revolutionary process. Socialist revolution could therefore break out in the weakest link of capitalism, Russia, and subsequently spread to the heartland of the capitalist system, the industrialised West. Using this explanatory framework, Lenin interpreted the February Revolution as meaning that the bourgeois revolution had 'to a certain extent' been completed, and that the task was now to push on to the socialist revolution. In practical terms, what this meant in April 1917 was a policy of no support for the Provisional Government, the taking of power by the soviets, the passing of the means

Red Guards protecting the Bolsheviks' headquarters at the Smolny Institute in Petrograd (David King Collection)

of production into the hands of the producers, and an immediate end to the war. These policy proposals were contained in Lenin's famous 'April Theses'.

Lenin's proposals, which ran directly counter to the views of the Party leadership in Russia, were initially widely opposed by both Party leaders and rank-and-file members. By virtue of his personal standing and ability, an appearance of compromise and the growing radicalisation of rank-and-file Party members, however, by mid-May Lenin had won Party support for his views. The Party now began publicly calling for 'All power to the soviets'. The aim of this policy seems to have been to push the moderate leaders of the Soviet further to the left and to encourage them to break the Soviet's links with the Provisional Government. If this proved impossible, these calls would highlight the weakness and compromising nature of the Petrograd Soviet. The policy thus seems to have been tactical rather than a result of any confidence that the Soviet might actually take power from the Provisional Government.

THE JULY DAYS

PROBLEMS AND ISSUES

• Role of the party; revolution

The Party leadership soon found itself lagging behind the popular mood. Under pressure from the rank-and-file, the Bolshevik leadership called a demonstration in Petrograd for 10 June. However, the First All-Russian Congress of Soviets (a meeting of representatives from soviets throughout Russia), which was meeting at that time, banned all demonstrations. The Bolshevik leadership, which recognised that the Party was not yet strong enough to defy the soviets, therefore cancelled the demonstration, to the disappointment of many of its followers. Three weeks later pressure built up again in the Bolsheviks' lower ranks, particularly in Party organisations in the military. The result was the July Days. This was an armed demonstration taking place on 3–4 July under the slogan 'All power to the soviets' and openly, if reluctantly, backed by the Bolshevik Central Committee (CC). The government, supported by the Petrograd Soviet, accused the party of planning a coup and took measures to suppress it. A number of Bolshevik leaders were arrested, Bolshevik newspapers were banned, and Lenin was forced to flee into hiding in Finland. Lenin now withdrew the slogan 'All power to the soviets'.

While this was clearly a setback for the Bolsheviks, the party continued to work away in the local organisations to consolidate its position among the working class. Although the trade unions remained predominantly under Menshevik influence, the Bolsheviks were able to expand their positions in the more radical factory committees and in many lower level soviets. Their success in this regard was aided by the Kornilov affair at the end of August.

Following the July Days, Lenin fled to Finland to avoid arrest by the government. To make good his escape, he was forced to shave and don a wig and working men's clothes (New York Public Library)

Review

- Put yourself in the position of a young Petrograd worker in July 1917. Write a paragraph explaining why you are about to join a protest march against the Provisional Government and why the Bolshevik party is increasingly attractive.

- How did Lenin change the Marxist theory of stages of development? Draw diagrams of the original theory (outlined in chapter 1) and Lenin's changes in 1917.

THE KORNILOV AFFAIR

PROBLEMS AND ISSUES

- Counter-revolution

Armed detachments of Bolshevik Red Guards, factory workers, students, soldiers and Baltic fleet sailors ranged the streets of Petrograd (UPI/ Bettmann)

In early and mid-August the commander-in-chief of the army General Lavr Kornilov had publicly urged a restoration of discipline on the home front (in the factories, on the streets and in the villages) as essential to maintaining the army as an effective fighting unit. This view was enthusiastically supported by conservative and many moderate elements of Russian society. Prime minister Kerensky also seemed to support this position, although his support was tempered by his suspicions about Kornilov's personal ambitions and his fear of a military coup. In any event, he seems to have agreed that Kornilov should lead some of his troops to Petrograd to put down the Bolshevik menace. Soon after Kornilov began his march on the capital, however, Kerensky accused him of attempting a coup and called on all to defend the government. As

a result, workers in the capital were armed, something which was rendered ultimately unnecessary by the disintegration of Kornilov's force before it reached Petrograd.

The Kornilov affair was an important turning point in the revolution. The growing sense of social crisis as popular unrest escalated during the summer had been met by government inaction. Its already low credibility was further eroded by the Kornilov affair. The government appeared unable to solve the problems facing Russia itself and unwilling to accept help from the military. But the failure of Kornilov's march on the capital also discredited another possible answer to the crisis: right-wing military government. The option of military rule, a common response to social unrest, seemed to disappear as a viable option with Kornilov's failure. This also helped to discredit the moderate leadership in the Petrograd Soviet because of the coalition arrangement between government and Soviet and because the Soviet had not been the main agency to organise defence of the revolution; the arming and organisation of the workers was carried out by those lower level organisations in which the Bolsheviks were becoming increasingly prominent.

PROBLEMS AND ISSUES

• Role of the party

If the Kornilov affair had discredited the right-wing military response to crisis and the moderate muddling-through approach of the Provisional Government and the Petrograd Soviet, the most likely option remaining was a radical left-wing approach. This was represented by the Bolsheviks, and it was this group which gained most from this affair. Bolshevik warnings about the likelihood of a coup seemed to have been borne out, and the Bolsheviks appeared to be the main defenders of the revolution. The growth in their support is reflected in the voting in local Duma elections in Moscow: between June and September the Bolshevik vote increased by about 164 per cent while that of the Kadets fell by 6 per cent, the SRs by 85 per cent and the Mensheviks by 79 per cent. On 31 August the Bolsheviks gained a majority in the Petrograd Soviet, followed five days later by a majority in the Moscow Soviet.

THE·SEIZURE OF POWER

PROBLEMS AND ISSUES

• Role of the party
• Revolution

Still in hiding, Lenin began to call upon the Bolshevik CC to make immediate preparations to seize power. There was strong opposition to this (see Case Study 2). On 10 October the decision was taken, in principle, to put the question of insurrection 'on the order of the day'. On 12 October a Military Revolutionary Committee was established in the Petrograd Soviet. This body, run by Trotsky, organised the actual mechanics of seizing power. The rising began on the evening of 24 October, was carried out by armed workers, soldiers and sailors, and proceeded with virtually no bloodshed and minimal opposition. There were no effective forces in the capital to defend the government, most of whose members were soon arrested; Kerensky escaped into exile.

On 25 October the Bolshevik leadership appeared before the Second All-Russian Congress of Soviets and announced the overthrow of the Provisional

The fighting was more prolonged in Moscow than in Petrograd in October–November 1917. This damage in central Moscow was caused by long-range artillery (L. Volkov-Lannit, Istoriia pishetsia ob'ektivom)

Government in the name of the Soviets. There was vigorous criticism of the Bolshevik action by many non-Bolshevik delegates who, in an act of folly, then withdrew from the Congress. The rump Congress, now overwhelmingly dominated by the Bolsheviks, proceeded to endorse an all-Bolshevik government headed by Lenin.

The Role of Lenin

The role Lenin played in the revolution has been a matter of debate for many years. Some, like E.H. Carr (*The Bolshevik Revolution 1917–1923*, London, Macmillan, 1953, Vol.1), have emphasised the part Lenin played in the unfolding of the Revolution and have seen him as the central influence shaping the Revolution. Other works have focused on social forces in the Revolution and have had very little to say about Lenin (e.g. S.A. Smith, *Red Petrograd. Revolution in the Factories, 1917–1918*, Cambridge, Cambridge University Press, 1983; Diane Koenker, *Moscow Workers and the 1917 Revolution*, Princeton, Princeton University Press, 1981; J.L.H. Keep, *The Russian Revolution. A Study in Mass Mobilization*, London, Weidenfeld & Nicolson, 1976; and Graeme J. Gill, *Peasants and Government in the Russian Revolution*, London, Macmillan, 1979). It is not that the latter deny Lenin a role in the Revolution, but they focus on aspects of the Revolution in which Lenin did not play a major part. But the question remains: what role did he play?

Clearly Lenin was very important. He was crucial to Bolshevik success. It was Lenin who changed Bolshevik policy in April and who persuaded the Party to seize power in October. Between April and October he was the Party's main spokesperson and the individual who did most to argue its policies and defend its positions. He was therefore partly responsible for the increase in the Bolsheviks' public profile and its consequent growth in support.

But this role must be seen in context. He did not organise the seizure of power. This was done by Leon Trotsky. Nor did he organise the Party in the working-class districts and factories of the capital. This was the task of numerous Party workers and officials working directly among the urban workers. Most importantly, he did not create the conditions that favoured the seizure of power by a radical group. These came about because the government could not meet the increasingly radical demands being made by a dissatisfied populace. It was the radicalisation of the different sections of the population, and the associated rejection of the authority of the centre and right of Russian politics, that created the conditions for the Bolshevik seizure of power. Lenin did contribute to this radicalisation by adopting radical positions during 1917, but the process of radicalisation had a logic of its own independent of Lenin. Thus although the Bolsheviks would not have seized power without Lenin, he could not have acted as he did unless the conditions had been favourable, and these were shaped largely by forces outside his control.

CASE STUDY 2

The Decision to Seize Power

PROBLEMS AND ISSUES
- Revolution
- Role of the party

The decision by the Bolsheviks to seize power is interesting not only because of the important consequences of that decision, but also because of what it tells us about Lenin's authority and position in the Party. A study of the course of the decision-making process shows that the Party was anything but the tightly organised, disciplined instrument of its leader.

Following the demonstration of the July Days and the Provisional Government's attempt to suppress the Bolsheviks, Lenin fled to Finland. He was to remain there, except for one visit to Petrograd in early October, until the eve of the takeover. As a result, most of his efforts to persuade the Central Committee (CC) to seize power had to be undertaken from afar, by letter. The preservation of these letters and of reports of CC deliberations and decisions enables us to follow the course of this process.

Throughout most of 1917, Lenin had been calling on the Soviet to take power into its own hands. He had dropped this call after the July Days when the Petrograd Soviet supported the government's attempts to suppress the Bolsheviks. Lenin was encouraged to call for the Bolsheviks to seize power in the wake of a revival of their fortunes following the Kornilov affair and the gaining of majorities in the Petrograd and Moscow Soviets.

In the period 12–14 September, Lenin wrote two letters to the CC. In the first, entitled 'The Bolsheviks must take power', Lenin declared:

> Now the Bolsheviks have a majority in the Soviets of Workers' and Soldiers' Deputies in both capitals, they can and *must* take state power into their own hands. They can, because the active majority of the revolutionary elements among the people in both the main cities is enough to fire the

masses, to overcome the resistance of the opposition and to smash it, to win power and to hold it. For, by offering a democratic peace straight away, by giving land to the peasants straight away, by restoring the democratic institutions and freedoms trampled on and crushed by Kerensky, the Bolsheviks will form a government that *no-one* will overthrow… Why is it now that the Bolsheviks must take power?

Because the impending surrender of Peter [Petrograd] will make our chances a hundred times worse. And while Kerensky and Co head the army, it is not in our power to prevent Peter's surrender. And we cannot 'wait for' the Constituent Assembly because Kerensky and Co, precisely by surrendering Peter, can always *block* it. Only our Party, once it has taken power, can ensure that the Constituent Assembly is called and once it has taken power, it will blame the other parties for putting it off and prove that accusation.

A separate peace between the British and German imperialists must and can be prevented but only by acting quickly.

The people are tired of the dithering by the Mensheviks and SRs. Our victory in the capitals is the only way to carry the peasants with us…

The point is to make the objective clear to the Party: an armed uprising in Peter and Moscow (with its region), the conquest of power and the overthrow of the government must go on the agenda…

It would be naive to wait for a 'formal' Bolshevik majority: no revolution waits for *that*… History will not forgive us if we do not take power now.

No apparatus? An apparatus exists: the Soviets and the democratic organisations…

By taking power both in Moscow and Peter *at once* (it doesn't matter which comes first, Moscow may possibly begin), we will win *absolutely and indisputably*.

Ann Bone (ed.). *The Bolsheviks and the October Revolution: Central Committee Minutes of the Russian Social Democratic Labour Party (Bolsheviks) August 1917–February 1918*, Pluto Press, London, 1974, pp.58–60

> **PROBLEMS AND ISSUES**
> • Ideology — in theory and practice

In the second letter, 'Marxism and Insurrection', Lenin defended preparation for an insurrection against the criticism that this was not Marxism but Blanquism*. He argued:

To be successful, insurrection must depend on the vanguard class, not on a conspiracy or a party. That is the first point. Insurrection must depend on a *revolutionary upsurge of the people*. That is the second point. Insurrection must depend on that *turning point* in the history of the mounting revolution when the advanced ranks of the people are at their most active and when the *vacillations* in the ranks of the enemy and *among the revolution's weak, half-hearted and irresolute friends* are at their most pronounced. That is the third point. These three conditions for raising the question of insurrection distinguish *Marxism* from *Blanquism*. But once these conditions are present, it is a betrayal of Marxism and a betrayal of the revolution to refuse to treat insurrection as *an art*.

Lenin, *Collected Works*, Vol.26, pp.22–7

* Blanquism is a theory stemming from the writings of French socialist Louis Blanqui. Its nucleus was the view that power could be seized by a small, conspiratorial minority of conscious revolutionaries acting independently of popular support.

Lenin then compared the situation prevailing at the time of the July Days with that at the time of his writing to try to show that 'the course of events has objectively put *insurrection* on the agenda'. He then suggested tactics that could be undertaken that would stay true to Marxism and advance the cause of insurrection.

Lenin's letters caused some concern in the CC, with members uncertain about how to react. Ultimately, as the minutes of the CC meeting of 15 September report, it decided:

> Comrade Kamenev moved the adoption of the following resolution: After considering Lenin's letter, the CC rejects the practical proposals they contain, calls on all organisations to follow CC instructions alone and affirms once again that the CC regards any kind of demonstration in the streets as quite impermissible at the present moment. At the same time, the CC makes a request to comrade Lenin to elaborate in a special brochure on the question he raised in his letters of a new assessment of the current situation and the Party's policy.
>
> The resolution is rejected. In conclusion, this decision is adopted: CC members in charge of work in the Military Organisation and the Petersburg Committee are instructed to take measures to prevent demonstrations of any kind in barracks and factories.

Bone, *Bolsheviks and the October Revolution*, p.58

This was a clear rejection of the line advocated by Lenin. The main problem for the CC was not whether insurrection was consistent with Marxism, but whether Lenin's evaluation of the contemporary situation was accurate: did Bolshevik majorities in the Petrograd and Moscow Soviets mean majority popular support for insurrection? Clearly, most members were dubious about this.

Lenin chafed at this rebuff, returning to his theme in a letter to I.T. Smilga written on 27 September. He reaffirmed the view that events compelled the party to 'put the armed uprising on the order of the day' (Lenin, *Collected Works*, Vol.26, pp.69–73). Two days later he wrote again to the CC, arguing that the outbreak of peasant revolt against the avowedly pro-peasant government led by the SRs was evidence that a crisis had matured in Russia. He also pointed to the radicalism of the representatives of the different nationalities of Russia and to the growth in Bolshevik support among the soldiers and the voters in Moscow. Lenin then urged action in the context of the current revolt in the German navy.

'The Crisis Has Matured', Lenin, *Collected Works*, Vol.26, pp.74–85

> To 'wait' for the Congress of Soviets and so forth under such circumstances would be a betrayal of internationalism, a betrayal of the cause of the world socialist revolution.

Failure to act would also constitute betrayal of the peasants. In a section of the letter that was not to be published, Lenin continued:

> ... there is a tendency, or an opinion, in our Central Committee and among the leaders of our Party which favours *waiting* for the Congress of Soviets, and is *opposed* to taking power immediately, is *opposed* to an immediate insurrection. That tendency, or opinion, must be overcome.

> Otherwise the Bolsheviks will cover themselves with eternal *shame* and *destroy themselves* as a party. For to miss such a moment and to 'wait' for the Congress of Soviets would be *utter idiocy* or *sheer treachery*. **"**

Lenin declared that the Bolsheviks had the armed support to succeed. He continued:

> **"** To refrain from taking power now, to 'wait', to indulge in talk in the Central Executive Committee, to confine ourselves to 'fighting for the organ' [of the Soviet], 'fighting for the Congress', is *to doom the revolution to failure*.
>
> In view of the fact that the Central Committee has *even left unanswered* the persistent demands I have been making for such a policy ever since the beginning of the Democratic Conference, in view of the fact that the Central Organ is deleting from my articles all references to such glaring errors on the part of the Bolsheviks as the shameful decision to participate in the Pre-Parliament, the admission of Mensheviks to the Presidium of the Soviet etc, etc. — I am compelled to regard this as a 'subtle' hint at the unwillingness of the Central Committee even to consider this question, a subtle hint that I should keep my mouth shut, and as a proposal for me to retire.
>
> I am compelled to *tender my resignation from the Central Committee*, which I hereby do, reserving for myself freedom to campaign among the *rank-and-file* of the Party and at the Party Congress.
>
> For it is my profound conviction that if we 'wait' for the Congress of Soviets and let the present moment pass, we shall *ruin* the revolution. **"**

In an article written at the same time, entitled 'Can the Bolsheviks Retain State Power?' (Lenin, *Collected Works*, Vol.26, pp.87–136), Lenin sought to show that all the anti-Bolshevik parties 'have admitted that the question of the Bolsheviks taking full state power alone is not only feasible, but also urgent'. Lenin then sought to rebut the view that if the proletariat seized power, it would be unable to retain it and exercise it effectively. In a 1 October letter to the CC, the Petrograd and Moscow Party committees and the Bolshevik members of the Petrograd and Moscow Soviets (Lenin, *Collected Works*, Vol.26, pp.140–1), Lenin reiterated his call for an immediate seizure of power and declared that procrastination and waiting were criminal.

While Lenin continued to press his point, the CC was coming under pressure from below as well, as the minutes of the meeting of 3 October suggest. Speaking of the report by Lomov about the situation in the Moscow region, the minute reads:

> **"** It becomes clear that the mood in the region is extremely tense. We have a majority in the Soviets in many places. The masses are putting forward the demand for concrete measures of some kind. Everywhere we are marking time. It is decided to have a debate on the report. **"**

Bone, *Bolsheviks and the October Revolution*, p.76

The following point in the minutes declared:

> **"** A decision is passed to suggest to Il'ich that he move to Peter to make close and constant contact possible. **"**

In accord with this decision, Lenin returned to Petrograd on 7 October, where he continued to press for a Bolshevik seizure of power.

On 10 October the CC met once again. Lenin repeated his arguments that the time was ripe and called on the CC to turn to the technical preparations for an uprising. A general discussion of the situation in the country preceded the adoption of the following resolution:

> The CC recognises that the international position of the Russian revolution (the insurrection in the German navy, an extreme sign of the way the world socialist revolution has grown through Europe; then the imperialists' threat of a peace aimed at stifling the revolution in Russia) as well as the military position (the decision undoubtedly made by the Russian bourgeoisie and Kerensky and Co to surrender Peter to the Germans) and the fact that the proletarian party has acquired a majority in the Soviets — all this taken together with the peasant revolt and the swing in popular confidence towards our Party (the Moscow elections) and finally the obvious preparations being made for a second Kornilov revolt (troops being withdrawn from Peter, cossacks moved towards Peter, Minsk encircled by cossacks etc) — all this puts an armed uprising on the order of the day.
>
> Recognising therefore that an armed rising is inevitable and that its time has come, the CC suggests that all Party organisations be guided by this and approach the discussion and solution of all practical issues from this point of view...

Bone, *Bolsheviks and the October Revolution*, pp.85–9

This resolution, which rehearsed the arguments Lenin had been advancing for the past four weeks, was not a clear commitment to insurrection. This question had been placed on 'the order of the day', but no effort was made to discuss the techniques or tactics whereby this could be realised. This reflects the continued level of uncertainty within the CC about this course of action.

The resolution had been adopted over the opposition of Zinoviev and Kamenev. Furthermore, of the 22 full members of the CC, nine were absent from this meeting. Of the missing members, Nogin, Rykov and Miliutin would probably have opposed this resolution, thereby giving an opposition bloc of almost a quarter of the committee. The next day in a statement to leading Party bodies, Zinoviev and Kamenev outlined their objections (Bone, *Bolsheviks and the October Revolution*, pp.89–95). They rejected Lenin's view that the majority of the populace and of the international proletariat had been won over to the Bolshevik side; the peasants supported the SRs and much soldier support would disappear if a proletarian government sought to mount a revolutionary war against German imperialism. Rather than insurrection, which would inevitably lead to defeat, the Bolsheviks should consolidate their position through the Congress of Soviets, due to meet on 20 October, and in the election to the Constituent Assembly.

At the CC meeting of 16 October, Lenin reaffirmed the arguments he had used earlier in getting the resolution of 10 October adopted. Reports followed, outlining the mood in various localities. Debate then took place about the question of insurrection, with some questioning the level of popular support Lenin believed the Bolsheviks had, and others reflecting a good deal of confusion about whether the 10 October resolution constituted a call for specific, immediate action on the part of the CC and the Bolsheviks. Following this debate, the meeting then adopted a resolution, moved by Lenin.

> 66 The meeting unreservedly welcomes and entirely supports the CC resolution, calls on all organisations and all workers and soldiers to make comprehensive and intensive preparations for an armed insurrection and to support the Centre created for this by the Central Committee and expresses its full confidence that the CC and the Soviet will be timely in indicating the favourable moment and the appropriate methods of attack. 99

Bone, *Bolsheviks and the October Revolution*, pp.96–109

This was adopted in principle by 20 votes to two with three abstentions. The meeting then appointed a Military Revolutionary Centre consisting of Sverdlov, Stalin, Bubnov, Uritsky and Dzerzhinsky to organise the rising.

In 'A Letter to Comrades' written on 17 October (Lenin, *Collected Works*, Vol.26, pp.195–215), Lenin vigorously rebutted the objections to an insurrection propounded by Zinoviev and Kamenev. On the following day, the non-Bolshevik newspaper *Novaia Zhizn'* published a statement by Kamenev in which he declared that:

> 66 I am not aware of any decisions by our Party which fix a rising of any sort for this or any other date... 99

Bone, *Bolsheviks and the October Revolution*, pp.121–2

and that

> 66 ... it would be inadmissible and fatal for the proletariat and the revolution for us to initiate an armed insurrection at the present moment... we believe that it is our duty now, in the present circumstances, to speak out against any attempt to initiate an armed insurrection which would be doomed to defeat and would bring in its train the most disastrous consequences for the Party, for the proletariat, for the revolution. 99

Lenin's response to this was vitriolic (Lenin, *Collected Works*, Vol.26, pp.216–19). Labelling Zinoviev and Kamenev strike-breakers, Lenin declared that he no longer considered them comrades and would fight to secure their expulsion from the Party. On the following day, Lenin, who was once again in hiding, penned a letter to the CC in which he called for the 'strike breaking... blacklegs' to be expelled from the Party (Lenin, *Collected Works*, Vol.26, pp.224–7). His letter was discussed at a meeting of the CC on 20 October, but among the variety of views there was little sympathy for his call for expulsion from the Party. Instead the meeting decided to accept Kamenev's resignation from the CC and to declare that Zinoviev and Kamenev 'were to refrain from any statements against the decisions of the CC and its projected line of work'.

On 24 October Lenin again called on his colleagues to carry out the rising and not to wait for the convocation of the Congress of Soviets, which had been postponed to 25 October (Lenin, *Collected Works*, Vol.26, pp.234–5). On the same day, the CC discussed organisational matters concerned with the insurrection (Bone, *Bolsheviks and the October Revolution*, pp.124–6). Although it seems to have discussed the question of the organisation of the insurrection at this meeting (and possibly that of 21 October), it is clear that organisation had been going on for some time. This was being done by the Military Revolutionary Committee of the Petrograd Soviet, a body dominated by Trotsky. It was this, not the Military Revolutionary Centre created by the CC, that was the real organiser of the insurrection. While this enabled the Bolsheviks to seize power under the fig-leaf of legitimacy provided by the Soviet, it may be reflective of the uncertainty within the CC that the actual preparations had to be made outside that body.

The picture that emerges from this tale is that Lenin had significant difficulty in persuading his colleagues to accept his view of the virtue of imminent insurrection. Some members of the committee, particularly Zinoviev and Kamenev, believed that he was far too optimistic in his assumptions about the level of popular support for the Bolsheviks. Others, in particular Trotsky, believed that the Bolsheviks should not attempt to seize power prior to the Congress of Soviets, but should time their actions in such a way as to cloak their accession to power in the semblance of legality provided by that body. What is clear is that the CC was not a body that was monolithic or a mere instrument of Lenin's will. It was a vibrant collection of individuals who retained a degree of independence of thought that was to be demonstrated repeatedly in the years immediately following 25 October 1917.

Review and discuss

- Who had the most influence on the course of events in 1917, Lenin, Trotsky, or Kerensky?

List of references

Geyer, Dietrich, *The Russian Revolution. Historical Problems and Perspectives*, Berg, Leamington Spa, 1987, ch. 8.

Harding, Neil, *Lenin's Political Thought. Vol. 2. Theory and Practice in the Socialist Revolution*, Macmillan, London, 1981, chs 6 & 7.

Pipes, Richard, *The Russian Revolution 1899–1919*, Knopf, New York, 1990, ch. 11.

Rabinowitch, Alexander, *The Bolsheviks Come to Power. The Revolution of 1917 in Petrograd*, W.W. Norton & Co., New York, 1978.

Reed, John, *Ten Days That Shook the World*, Penguin, Harmondsworth, 1966 (originally published 1926), ch. 3.

Essay Questions

1 Compare and contrast the February and the October Revolutions of 1917: what roles were played by (a) mass participation, and (b) calculating political leadership in each of those episodes?

2 'The Provisional Government's determination that Russia continue to participate in World War I diverted its attention from desperately needed domestic reforms and thereby made its eventual fall inevitable.' How valid is this assessment?

3 'Society was so divided by radical attitudes that the prospects of a moderate government surviving, let alone asserting itself, were very slim: it was a situation ready made for a seizure of power by either right- or left-wing extremists.' Does the evidence support this assessment of the situation in Russia in 1917?

4 'Increasing popular radicalism rather than the leadership provided by politicians was crucial in determining the course of events in Russia during 1917.' How valid is this assessment?

5 Was the October Revolution of 1917 a genuine revolution with substantial mass support, or was it simply a *coup d'état*, i.e. a seizure of power by a relatively small armed group?

THE CONSOLIDATION OF POWER

CHAPTER THREE

1917–21

THE BOLSHEVIKS came to power in Russia with the support of a substantial minority of the population. They had to set about building up their power and consolidating their authority under very difficult conditions.

Focus questions

Some of the important factors in the Bolsheviks' eventual success may be understood in considering the following questions:

- How was the single party state brought into existence?

- What was War Communism?
- What was the fate of opposition in the party during this period?
- Why was the New Economic Policy introduced? How did it differ from War Communism?

The toppling of the Provisional Government meant that the Bolsheviks held power in the capital while claiming authority over the country as a whole. It was to be three years, however, before that claim could be enforced throughout Russia. Moscow and most of the other major urban centres were controlled by local Bolshevik forces within a few weeks of the events in Petrograd, but it was to take much longer for control to penetrate the countryside. The Bolsheviks remained a party of the cities. This was ably demonstrated by the results of the election to the Constituent Assembly.

This poster by A. Apsit was published by the All-Union Central Executive Committee to celebrate the first year of proletarian dictatorship (Sovietsky Khudoznik Publishers, Moscow)

THE CONSTITUENT ASSEMBLY ELECTION

In the period before its fall, the Provisional Government had finally set in train the organisational arrangements for a national election for the Constituent Assembly. When the Bolsheviks came to power, despite some reluctance by Lenin to adhere to the commitment to hold this election, they felt they had no choice but to allow the election to proceed. The share of votes and of delegates for the major parties is shown in the table below.

Table 3.1 Results of the Election to the Constituent Assembly

	Percentage of votes	Number of seats
Right SRs	38	370
Bolsheviks	24	175
Left SRs (see below)	—	40
Kadets	5	17
Mensheviks	3	16

The split in the Socialist Revolutionary Party did not occur in time for the Right and Left SRs to offer separate lists of candidates. The proportion of Left SR votes is therefore included within those for the Right SRs.

Most of the other delegates were from national parties. The total number of delegates was 707. The vast majority of peasants had supported the SRs, presumably disassociating the party from the discredited Provisional Government. The Bolsheviks received their support from among the urban workers and the soldiers, especially those in Moscow and Petrograd. The election clearly demonstrated the urban nature of Bolshevik support and the fact that less than a quarter of the population had been willing to vote for them in a free election.

The urban nature of Bolshevik support was consistent with the party's basic outlook and orientation. Ideologically, it placed overwhelming importance on the urban working class, which was seen as the hope of the future. In contrast, the peasantry constituted a backward class that could play an important role under proletarian leadership in the revolution, but was ultimately doomed to disappear in the course of historical development. This anti-peasant ideological bias was matched by very limited direct knowledge of the conditions of peasant life. Most leading Bolsheviks were not from among the peasantry (Mikhail Kalinin, future Soviet president, was an exception) and they had very little appreciation of the realities of peasant life. Their inability to come to grips with life in the countryside was to be reflected in future policy positions.

With only minority support in the country, and soon confronted by an imposing array of enemies, how did the Bolsheviks consolidate and stabilise their rule? Three areas of activity are important in this: the establishment of the single party state and the defeat of opposition, reconciliation with the population, and the structuring of the regime itself.

PROBLEMS AND ISSUES

- Ideology — in theory and practice

THE SINGLE PARTY STATE

The government Lenin presented to the Second All-Russian Congress of Soviets on the evening of 25 October was all-Bolshevik in composition. This was unacceptable both to elements in the party (five people, Zinoviev, Kamenev, Rykov, Nogin and Miliutin, resigned from the CC in protest) and to socialist forces in Russia as a whole. Under pressure from within the party and, more importantly, from the Executive Committee of the All-Russian Union of Railwaymen (*Vikzhel*), Lenin agreed to the formation of a coalition government. The only party willing to enter a coalition arrangement, and that was acceptable to Lenin, was the Left SRs. Accordingly on 17 November, a coalition government between the two parties was formed; seven Left SRs entered the Council of People's Commissars (*Sovnarkom*), while others took up leading roles in the government commissariats (ministries). The basis of unity between the two parties was weak, however. The coalition collapsed when the Left SRs walked out of the government on 19 March 1918 in protest at the signing of the Brest-Litovsk peace treaty with Germany (see p.72). Henceforth, the Bolsheviks were the only party in government.

PROBLEMS AND ISSUES

● Role of the party and the state

The Demise of the Opposition

The consolidation of single party rule involved the elimination of, as far as possible, all alternative independent channels of political activity. By mid-1918 the three main alternative parties, the Kadets, SRs and Mensheviks, had been subjected to 'administrative measures' that involved the arrest of party leaders, the closure of party presses, and the effective break-up of the parties. During the Civil War, these parties led a shadowy existence; although at times they seemed to be semi-rehabilitated, their political life in Russia was effectively at an end. They were finally shattered in 1921 and 1922 following the introduction of the New Economic Policy (NEP). Never again were they serious actors on the Russian stage. Their demise, which did not lead to widespread popular protest, should not have been unexpected. The Kadets, the SRs and the Left SRs had all advocated the armed overthrow of the Bolsheviks, a course of action that would have led to their suppression in most political systems. Although the Mensheviks had not formally adopted such a course, their complete hostility to the government was unlikely to earn them favourable treatment.

Restructuring the Political Arena

The elimination of alternative parties was accompanied by the restructuring of the political arena within which any competitive party system would have been likely to operate. The Constituent Assembly seemed to pose a major problem for the Bolsheviks. Before October 1917, all socialist groups including the Bolsheviks had agreed that only such a body could take the crucial decisions about the future course of Russian development. So important had the

Constituent Assembly been considered, that the Bolsheviks were not game to cancel the election for this body after they had seized power. But when the Assembly met on the evening of 5–6 January 1918, it was dispersed by the Bolsheviks with a minimum of force and no meaningful opposition. The first body in Russian history elected on a truly democratic franchise with a real choice of candidates ceased to exist with hardly a murmur of opposition. The official reason given for its dismissal was that the election which had been held in November did not represent the political realities and conditions of post-October Russia.

The other institution in which political parties might have been able to act was the soviets. As a result of both a surge of popular support for the Bolsheviks and organisational manipulation by Bolshevik activists, soviets throughout the country fell under the control of their executive committees. Increasingly these came under Bolshevik domination. Although these trends were not uniform in all parts of the country, they nevertheless proceeded with a seeming inevitability. The whole soviet apparatus began losing the independence from the governing structure that had been the keystone of its existence from the beginning.

Review and discuss

- Discuss the results of the Constituent Assembly election, and consider what role the Constituent Assembly could have played if it had proceeded.

THE CIVIL WAR

The biggest threat to the Bolsheviks during this period came from military developments. The first threat came from the German army, but this was soon neutralised by the Treaty of Brest-Litovsk in March 1918 (see p.72). Three months later, the Bolsheviks found themselves at war with a foe that controlled large parts of Russia itself. The enemy consisted of armed forces raised chiefly by former officers in the tsarist army, the so-called Whites. They were aided by a number of foreign powers, including Britain, Japan, France and the USA, who committed troops to the Russian Civil War. Although the various groups that comprised the anti-Bolshevik forces may have differed in their attitude to the restoration of the monarchy, they were united in their desire to overthrow the Bolsheviks. These forces advanced from various directions on the capital, Moscow, and steadily compressed the Bolshevik-controlled area until it reached approximately the dimensions of old Muscovy. The situation seemed dark for the Bolsheviks.

PROBLEMS AND ISSUES

- Counter-revolution

*The Civil War
(adapted from Martin
McCauley (ed.).
Russian Revolution
and the Soviet State,
1917–21, Macmillan,
London, 1975, p.90)*

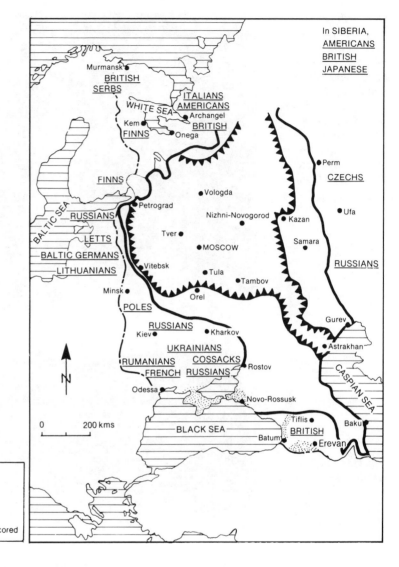

In SIBERIA,
AMERICANS
BRITISH
JAPANESE

Murmansk
BRITISH
SERBS
ITALIANS
AMERICANS
WHITE SEA Archangel
Kem BRITISH
FINNS Onega
Perm
CZECHS
FINNS
Vologda
Petrograd Nizhni-Novogorod Ufa
RUSSIANS Kazan
Tver Samara
LETTS MOSCOW
BALTIC SEA
BALTIC GERMANS Vitebsk RUSSIANS
LITHUANIANS Tula
Minsk Tambov
Orel
POLES Gurev
RUSSIANS Astrakhan
Kiev Kharkov
UKRAINIANS
RUMANIANS COSSACKS
FRENCH RUSSIANS Rostov CASPIAN SEA
Odessa
Novo-Rossusk
0   200 kms Tiflis Baku
BLACK SEA BRITISH
Batum Erevan

Remnant of anti-Bolshevik activity, 1920–21
Under Bolshevik rule, November 1918
Maximum advance of anti-Bolshevik forces
Russian frontier, March 1921
Principal armies are in capital letters, underscored

Trotsky and the Red Army

The Bolsheviks were able to break out of this ring and defeat their enemies. They had the real advantage of internal lines of communication compared with the over-extended lines in use by the Whites. This created problems of co-ordination for the White leaders. This problem was compounded by the high levels of disorganisation in White ranks, the conflicts and disputes between White leaders, and their inability to gain widespread popular support. Despite popular reservations about the Bolsheviks resulting from their economic policies (see pp.65–7) and from the use of the so-called Red Terror to get rid of enemies, most people associated the Whites with tsarism and saw the Bolsheviks as the better of two evils. But also crucial to Bolshevik success was the organisational role played by Trotsky. Through his energy, organisational skills and force of personality, Trotsky built up the Red Army from

One of the reasons for the Bolshevik success in the Civil War was the performance of the Red Army. Leon Trotsky, shown here addressing some troops, was the main organiser and leader of the army (New York Public Library)

The tsar and his family were executed by local zealots in Ekaterinburg in the Ural Mountains on the night of 16–17 July 1918. Before being moved to Ekaterinburg, they were kept in the west Siberian town of Tobolsk (BBC Hulton Picture Library, London)

nothing to a powerful military machine. Many workers from the cities joined the Red Army. Victories on the battlefield by Trotsky's forces plus the internal weaknesses of the Whites ultimately led to Bolshevik victory and the expulsion of the Whites from Russia. By the end of 1920, and following an unsuccessful Bolshevik invasion of Poland in an attempt to spark revolution there, the fighting was ended.

The Civil War was very important for the Bolsheviks because it reinforced their belief in the justness and inevitability of their cause. It confirmed their views about the hostility to the Revolution on the part of capitalist forces. It also provided an opportunity for the killing of the tsar and his family, thereby eliminating a potential rallying point for anti-Bolshevik forces.

If the victory in October 1917 had been quick and relatively easy, that of the Civil War was not. It had a militarising and brutalising effect on the new regime as well as providing it with a real boost to morale and a reinforced sense of commitment. It was important, too, for popular support, and it is to this that we must now turn.

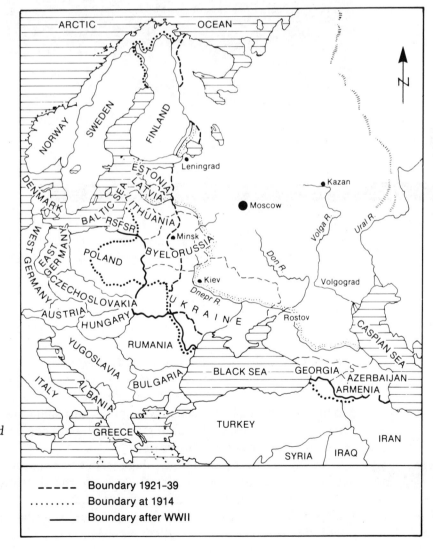

The western boundary between the Soviet Union and neighbouring countries in Europe after World War II. Map shows western border in 1921–39 and in 1914 (before World War I)

- - - - - Boundary 1921–39
·········· Boundary at 1914
——— Boundary after WWII

In the early years of Bolshevik rule, extensive efforts were made to spread their message to all corners of the country. One means of doing this was through brightly coloured propaganda trains. The picture on this train shows the defence of the citadel of Russia against the many-headed dragon of imperialism (UPI/ Bettmann)

RELATIONS WITH THE POPULACE

After ousting the Provisional Government in October 1917, the Bolsheviks sought to broaden their basis of support. To achieve this, they introduced a number of decrees granting the people what they had been demanding. Decrees were adopted passing land into the hands of those who cultivated it and establishing workers' control in industrial, commercial and banking enterprises with more than five employees. The government immediately offered an armistice and peace negotiations based on the principle of 'no annexations and indemnities'. Independence was formally granted to Poland and Finland, and the right of national self-determination confirmed in principle. Although many of these measures merely ratified the existing situation, they signalled to the population that the new regime was intent on responding to their concerns. They were also means of building up popular support. That support was to be sorely tested in the coming years.

Initial moves in the economic sphere were somewhat hesitant. They reflect neither an attempt to move directly towards the construction of socialism, nor the implementation of a clearly defined blueprint for change. The Bolshevik leadership saw its task as a holding operation; they had to ensure that the Revolution survived until socialist revolution in the advanced capitalist West

PROBLEMS
AND ISSUES

● Ideology — in
  theory and
  practice

created conditions for the worldwide advance to socialism. Only in the context of worldwide socialism could socialism in Russia be achieved. Given this view of Russia's inability to proceed to socialism alone, the measures the government adopted nationalising the banks, foreign trade and some enterprises and formally establishing collectivised agriculture were ad hoc and motivated by immediate political concerns, not an ideologically based attempt to build socialism.

WAR COMMUNISM

The outbreak of the Civil War in the middle of 1918 led to a major change in economic policy. This was the introduction of War Communism. Some have suggested that this policy was an attempt by the Bolsheviks to leap straight into socialism; even if ultimate success did depend on socialism being achieved in the West, significant steps in a socialist direction could be taken in Russia in the interim. But it is more likely that War Communism was a reaction to the wartime conditions that was justified in ideological terms. It was then pushed to extremes not originally envisaged by those more radical elements among the Bolsheviks who wished to hasten the move to socialism. It made no sense to try to build socialism in the middle of a civil war, but elements of War Communism were clearly compatible with the operation of a wartime economy. This is discussed in Case Study 3.

The main element of War Communism was the establishment of centralised control over all production and distribution. This included:
- the compulsory delivery of grain to the state;
- the nationalisation of all industry (small scale industry was not nationalised until November 1920);
- a ban on private trade;
- a rationing system of food and consumer goods.

Money lost all value and in many areas ceased to act as a medium of exchange; barter frequently took its place. Wages and salaries were paid in kind. This was the first time in the Union of Soviet Socialist Republics that an attempt had been made to introduce a command economy, that is, an economy that was to be driven by state direction rather than market forces.

Food Shortages and the Black Market

The policies of War Communism in a society already suffering from three and a half years of war against the Germans, the Revolution and the Civil War, created real difficulties for the populace. In the Civil War the peasantry seem to have supported the Bolsheviks against the opposing White forces, which were seen as representing a return to the old system and the loss of the land peasants had only just acquired. But the peasantry opposed the policies of War Communism. Just as in 1917, there was no incentive for producers to surrender their grain to the state. As a result there were widespread food shortages in the cities and clashes in the countryside between peasant producers and armed requisitioning squads from the cities. (This became part of the Red Terror and the opposing White Terror.) Black markets flourished for all goods, and many in the cities were kept alive only through the efforts of the notorious 'bagmen' who carried food into the cities for private, illegal sale. The shortage of food was accompanied by epidemics of typhus, cholera and scarlet fever. An indication of conditions in the cities is given by the following extract, dating from October 1918:

> Famine is rife in Petrograd, and it is a common occurrence when a horse falls down in the street for the people to rush out of the houses to cut off the flesh of the animal the moment it has breathed its last. My informant has also seen lying in the street the carcass of a horse, the head and shoulders of which had been cut off for food. The peasants refuse to sell food for money, but are ready to barter it for clothes, boots, furniture; the shops are all empty...
>
> Money is paid out at the banks in an absolutely arbitrary way to those who have deposits, but by heavy bribes it is possible to get out larger sums. Until quite recently people sold their possessions: *objets d'art*, jewellery, pictures, furniture — either privately or deposited them in commission shops where they were bought by wealthy Jews, rich speculators and affluent working people. Now, however, no furniture may be sold as it has been declared the common property of the nation, just as all house property has been nationalised, the rents being paid to the Bolshevik Government. People are no longer permitted to take any furniture with them if they leave their flats, and they are often compelled to leave their homes because these have been commandeered by the Bolsheviks; and on nearly every family Red Guards have been quartered. At one time blankets were requisitioned, and every bourgeois family was compelled to hand over one good woollen blanket, ostensibly for the Red Guards, but it was common knowledge that they were being sold to the Germans.
>
> Unless people had about 1000 roubles (£100) a month per person, they had to starve, and even these favoured ones had to satisfy their hunger with the following food: a certain kind of dried fish, which had to be soaked for 24 hours before it could be boiled; flour, buckwheat and other cereals at 30/- a pound; potatoes, five twice a week, at 6/6 or 7/- a lb. The peel of the potatoes is minced, mixed with breadcrumbs and made into rissoles. In order to buy these vegetables one has to go in the early hours of the morning to a certain market. Another way of getting food was by buying it at exorbitant prices from members of the Red Guards who are well-fed. Many people, who are not Bolsheviks, have joined the Red Guards for the sake of the food given them. Lenin and his colleagues are living in affluence.

Sir B. Pares, Personal Papers, Martin McCauley (ed.), *The Russian Revolution and the Soviet State 1917–1921 Documents*, Macmillan, London, 1975, pp.278–9

These conditions contributed substantially to the depopulation of the cities at this time. Many urban inhabitants sought to escape the hardship by moving to the countryside, perhaps to live with relations or to take up again the places in the villages that they may have left less than a generation ago. Although the figures are, at best, an approximation, it was estimated in December 1920 that since 1917 the population of 40 provincial capitals had fallen by 33 per

PROBLEMS AND ISSUES

● Counter-revolution

During the famine of 1920-21, cannibalism appeared in parts of the stricken areas. A business grew up in the sale of bodies to the starving. The picture shows some of these traders (Imperial War Museum, London)

cent, of 50 other large towns by 16 per cent, and of Moscow and Petrograd by 44.5 and 57.5 per cent respectively. This melting away of the urban proletariat was a serious problem for the Bolsheviks because it represented the erosion of their ideological basis and their main source of social support. Furthermore, this occurred in a context of widespread peasant hostility, which was reflected in the withholding of grain and the outbreak of armed uprisings in different parts of Russia. The most serious of these were in Tambov province, Ukraine and Western Siberia in 1920. Strike activity was significant in the cities, and in February-March 1921 the sailors in the naval base of Kronstadt near Petrograd rebelled.

The Kronstadt rebellion was particularly serious because sailors in Kronstadt had been solid supporters of the Bolsheviks in 1917. Their rebellion was seen not just as a reflection of opposition to current policies, but a challenge to the whole of the Revolution. Kronstadt showed the depth of opposition the Bolsheviks' policies had aroused. Their opposition rested on a sense of the betrayal of the Revolution and its ideals. For this reason, Bolshevik leaders recognised that the rebellion had to be crushed. In March, Trotsky led loyal troops across the frozen sea to the naval base, and vigorously suppressed the rebels.

- In light of the policies adopted by the Bolshevik government, draft an appeal for the support of the populace during the war.

THE NEW ECONOMIC POLICY

PROBLEMS AND ISSUES

- Ideology — in theory and practice

Faced with such widespread social dislocation and unrest, the Bolsheviks were forced to compromise. This took the form of the New Economic Policy (NEP), introduced at the Tenth Congress of the Communist Party in March 1921. The NEP was a retreat from the extensive state control of the economy under War Communism. Although the state retained control of the 'commanding heights' of the economy (large-scale industry, banking and foreign trade) much wholesale trade, large shops and other enterprises were passed back into private hands. Small manufacturing concerns, artisans and craftsmen were once again encouraged. But most importantly, state control of the grain trade was abolished; a set rate of tax was imposed on the peasants who were allowed to dispose of their post-tax grain surplus in whatever way they wished. The basic principle whereby the economy was to function was the operation of market forces, and even state enterprises had to operate according to market principles of profit and loss. Levels of central planning were reduced, with plans becoming guidelines instead of compulsory instructions. The currency was stabilised on the gold standard and government spending reduced.

The introduction of the NEP was a clear admission by the Bolsheviks that they could not exercise control over the countryside. The Bolsheviks' weakness in the face of the peasantry was clearly acknowledged by Lenin in his explanation for the introduction of the new measures:

> We know that so long as there is no revolution in other countries, only agreement with the peasantry can save the socialist revolution in Russia. And that is how it must be stated, frankly, at all meetings and in the entire press. We know that this agreement between the working class and the peasantry is not solid — to put it mildly, without entering the word 'mildly' in the minutes — but, speaking plainly it is very much worse. Under no circumstances must we try to hide anything; we must plainly state that the peasantry is dissatisfied with the form of our relations, that it does not want relations of this type and will not continue to live as it has hitherto. This is unquestionable. The peasantry has expressed its will in this respect definitely enough. It is the will of the vast masses of the working population. We must reckon with this, and we are sober enough politicians to say frankly: let us re-examine our policy in regard to the peasantry. The state of affairs that has prevailed so far cannot be continued any longer...
>
> We must try to satisfy the demands of the peasants who are dissatisfied and disgruntled, and legitimately so, and who cannot be otherwise. We must say to them: 'Yes, this cannot go on any longer.' How is the peasant to be satisfied and what does satisfying him mean? Where is the answer? Naturally it lies in the demands of the peasantry. We know these demands. But we must verify them and examine all that we know of the farmer's economic demands from the standpoint of economic science. If we go into this, we shall see at once that it will take essentially two things to satisfy the small farmer. The first is a certain freedom of exchange, freedom for the small private proprietor, and the second is the need to obtain commodities and produce.

'Report on the Substitution of a Tax in Kind for the Surplus-Grain Appropriation System, March 15', Lenin, *Collected Works*, Vol.32, pp.215–17

This anonymous poster from 1920 calls on all to remember the heroic days of October and declares that the RSFSR has the support of the workers and peasants of the world (Sovietsky Khudoznik Publishers, Moscow)

Discuss

- What sort of symbolism is evoked in this poster?

- How does this poster fit in with the sort of conditions described in the extract from Sir Bernard Pares on p.66?

Just as in 1917 the peasants had rejected the authority of the government and thereby contributed to its fall, so in the period of War Communism the peasants had demonstrated the limits of the government's power. That power did not extend far outside the urban areas, and the solidity of its position within the towns was also shaky. This was a lesson that was to have echoes later in the decade. Furthermore, during this period the Bolsheviks demonstrated that they had little accurate knowledge of, or sensitivity to, the peasantry. With the policy of War Communism, including the futile attempt to incite class war in the villages by the establishment of poor peasants' committees in 1918, the urban-based Bolsheviks showed their lack of understanding of the principles of the peasant economy and the nature of peasant life.

Discuss

- How do the policies of War Communism and NEP compare with traditional notions of socialism?

Review

- How did the Civil War affect support for the Bolsheviks?
- In what ways was the working class affected by the Civil War, and how did this affect the Bolshevik government?

STRUCTURING THE REGIME

PROBLEMS AND ISSUES

- Role of the party and state

When the Bolsheviks came to power they had no clearly formulated ideas about how the new regime might be structured. As we have already seen, the establishment of a single party system had led to a split in the Bolshevik leadership. After the Left SRs walked out of the government in March 1918 over the Brest-Litovsk peace treaty issue, however, opposition to single party rule within the leadership collapsed. More generally, the Bolsheviks had no agreed blueprint about how the new regime would operate; institutions developed and relations between them were worked out as they went along.

Formally the Council of Peoples' Commissars, or *Sovnarkom*, was responsible to the All-Russian Congress of Soviets and, between Congresses, to its Central Executive Committee. But this formal responsibility was never realised in practice, and from its establishment when the Bolsheviks took power, *Sovnarkom* was the real seat of government. Throughout the early years of Bolshevik rule, the dominant place the Party was to occupy in the Soviet system was not yet in evidence. At least until 1919, *Sovnarkom* and its executive organs, the Little *Sovnarkom* and the Defence Council (later Labour and Defence Council), all of which were dominated by Lenin personally, rivalled the Party's CC as the single most important institution of Bolshevik rule. But from 1919 the prominence of *Sovnarkom* was eroded and the bodies at the apex of the Party structure became dominant.

Systematisation of the Party

One of the main reasons for the decline of *Sovnarkom* was the systematisation of bodies at the top of the Party structure. This took place at the Eighth Congress

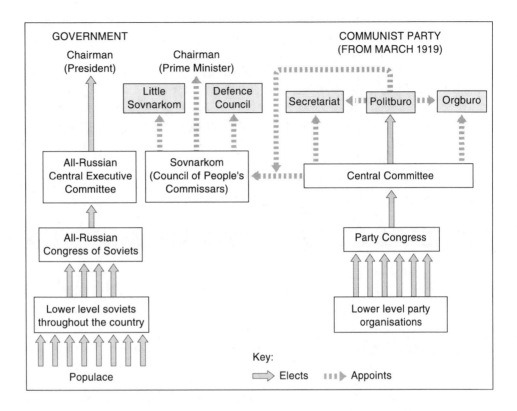

of the Party in March 1919. This meeting formally created three new executive organs for the party:

The Political Bureau, or Politburo: The task of this body was to deal with urgent matters that could not wait for the next meeting of the CC. Because the CC had the right to exercise the powers of the supreme policy-making body of the Party (the Congress) between Congresses, and the Politburo could exercise the powers of the CC between meetings of that body, the Politburo had enormous power in the day-to-day operations of the Party. The regularity of the Politburo's meetings and its small size gave it a decided advantage over the CC and were major reasons why, over time, it was able to displace the CC as the most powerful body in the Party. If the Politburo was envisaged as a decision-making organ, the other two bodies established at this time were to be administrative organs.

The Organisational Bureau, or Orgburo: According to the Congress resolution that created this body, the Orgburo 'directs all the organisational work of the Party' (Vos'moi s'ezd RKP(b). Mart 1919 goda. Protokoly, Moscow, 1959, p.425). In theory, this body was to be responsible for making the most important administrative and personnel decisions in the Party.

The Secretariat: This body was to implement decisions of the Orgburo and do the necessary preparatory work for sessions of the Politburo.

The distinctions between these bodies were in principle quite clear, but in practice their activities overlapped considerably. Moreover the potential power that lay in these organs was considerable: between the Politburo and the Orgburo, all major questions of policy and personnel were likely to arise. As the only full (voting) member of both bodies, Stalin was well placed to take full advantage of this (see Case Study 4).

Prior to the establishment of these organs in 1919, the most important Party body was the CC. It was the CC that decided on the seizure of power in October and it was here that all major questions came up for discussion. But during this period the CC had to share this role with the Party Congress, which, in sharp contrast to its purely ritualised role later in Soviet history, played a real part in the decision-making process. This was in part a result of intra-party conflict at the time.

MAJOR DEBATES IN THE COMMUNIST PARTY

The Left Communists and Brest-Litovsk

The first main bout of political conflict following the dispute over the coalition government concerned the Brest-Litovsk peace treaty with the Germans. The Bolsheviks had come to power on a peace platform, but the problem was how peace could best be achieved. Negotiations with Germany continued incon-clusively for some time, with the Germans exerting increased pressure in February 1918 by breaking the armistice and renewing their advance into Russia. The Party leadership was split into three groups over this issue:

- Trotsky, the main negotiator at the peace talks, supported a strategy of 'no war, no peace'. This amounted to a refusal both to continue the war and to sign an unacceptable peace.
- Lenin favoured signature of a peace treaty regardless of the terms it might involve. He believed that the Russian army was in no state to defend the country against the Germans, and that in any case concessions and com-promises would be temporary because workers' revolution in Germany was imminent.
- Nikolai Bukharin and the so-called Left Communists (supported by the coalition partners, the Left SRs) rejected any thought of a peace treaty and believed that what was necessary was to mount a revolutionary war against the Germans. They believed that this would ignite revolution in Germany, and thence in Europe.

The debate on this issue was conducted both in the CC, where even Lenin's threat to resign did not secure majority support for his position, and in the party at large. Speakers supporting the different sides toured the country addressing Party meetings. Their aim was to win over Party opinion so that delegates supporting their view would be elected to the extraordinary Seventh Congress of the Party that was to meet in March 1918 to resolve this question. As the debate raged and the consequences of following the path of revolutionary war and of adopting Trotsky's position of neither war nor peace became clear to all, support for Lenin's position grew. When the Congress met, it endorsed

Lenin's line and the punitive peace demanded by the Germans, which involved the Russian surrender of much territory including most of Ukraine, was signed. The effect of this treaty was limited in practice because of the defeat of the Germans a few months later. The Left Communists were shattered by this decision, however. They remained in existence for some time after March 1918, extending their criticism to various aspects of Soviet domestic policy, but disappeared as a distinct grouping by about the middle of the year.

The Military Opposition

PROBLEMS
AND ISSUES
• Ideology — in
theory and
practice

At the following Congress, the Eighth in March 1919, another opposition group emerged. This was the Military Opposition, based principally in the Party organs in the military, which opposed the policies of centralisation and discipline Trotsky had used (with CC approval) to build the army. The Military Opposition favoured an army based on militia and guerrilla forces with elected officers. Although this policy was consistent with pre-October views, it was unable to capture much support in the Party as a whole, particularly in the current wartime conditions. It was rejected by the Congress.

The Struggle for Democracy

Two other opposition groups emerged at this time and remained active into 1921. These were the Workers' Opposition and the Democratic Centralists. The Workers' Opposition was based in the trade unions and consisted largely of members of the proletariat, although its leader was the very unproletarian Alexandra Kollontai. The Workers' Opposition criticisms stemmed from an initial concern with the way that workers' interests were being sacrificed by the Party in the interests of the elite. This concern was soon widened to embrace a critique of the whole course of Soviet development. They attacked the growing isolation of the Party leaders from the rank-and-file workers who comprised the Party membership, and the way the powers of the leaders were expanding at the expense of the initiative and activity of the workers. They called this process 'bureaucratisation' and believed it could be overcome only through the restoration of democratic principles in Party life. More specifically they called for filling offices by election rather than appointment from above, the implementation of widespread rank-and-file debate on all issues before decisions were taken, and the expansion of the local initiative of workers.

These sorts of criticisms were also made by the Democratic Centralists. Mainly of non-proletarian background, many of the Democratic Centralists were former Left Communists, and their criticisms echoed many of the points made at the time of Brest-Litovsk. Their criticisms were mainly about the disappearance of democracy inside the Party. They argued that power had become concentrated in Party leaders at the expense of the rank-and-file and of those Party bodies that were supposed to exercise real power. They called for an end to the practice of filling positions by appointment and the restoration of elections, the reanimation of Party committees as effective working bodies

Alexandra Kollontai with delegates to the International Communist Women's Conference in Moscow, 1921. Kollontai became leader of the Workers Opposition (UPI/ Bettmann)

at all levels, and the accountability of leading organs to the rank-and-file. Bureaucratism could be overcome only through increased democracy.

The Trade Union Debate

The fate of these two opposition groups was bound up with the trade union discussion that split the Party in 1920–21. The question of the role the trade unions should play in the economy had been simmering in these years. The main point at issue was whether the trade unions should directly control the economy, as the Workers' Opposition demanded, or whether they should become an integral part of the party-state structure, as Lenin desired. The inability of the CC to reach agreement on this issue led to its being thrown open to Party-wide debate. As part of this discussion it was decided that delegates to the forthcoming Tenth Congress of the Party should be elected on the basis of which platform on this issue they supported. This meant that the strength of opposition to Lenin's view crystallised as Party members were forced to reveal their positions publicly. It also meant that there was open competition between factional groups for the support of rank-and-file party members. The result of this shadow of electoral competition was overwhelming support for Lenin's position, which was adopted at the Congress.

THE TENTH CONGRESS

This Congress was very important in the history of the Party because of the decisions it made about opposition in Party ranks. Up until this time, the right to oppose and criticise Party leaders had been an acknowledged right of all Party members. Now, under the impact of the trade union discussion, peasant risings and the Kronstadt rebellion, Lenin introduced two resolutions at the Congress that directly affected this right. One, entitled 'The Syndicalist and Anarchist Deviation in Our Party' roundly criticised the Workers' Opposition and linked their activity to the 'petit bourgeois' opposition in the country at large. The second resolution, 'On Party Unity', was wider in scope. This resolution defined fractions as 'groups with special platforms which to a certain extent aimed at closing ranks and creating their own discipline', and, having noted the presence of a number of these in the Party, called for their immediate dissolution on pain of expulsion:

PROBLEMS AND ISSUES

- Ideology — in theory and practice
- Role of the party

> It is essential that all politically conscious workers should clearly understand the danger and impermissibility of any fractionalism whatsoever which inevitably will lead in fact to the weakening of harmonious work and to the intensified and repeated attempts by enemies who have attached themselves to the ruling party to deepen the division and utilise it for counter-revolution... Congress orders the immediate dispersal of all groups, without exception, which were based on some platform or other, and instructs all organisations to take the greatest care not to permit any fractional speeches. Failure to execute this resolution of the congress must result in the unconditional and immediate expulsion from the party.

Desiatyi s'ezd RKP(b) Mart 1921 goda: Stenograficheskii otchet, Moscow, 1963, pp.571–6

All fractions in the Party were henceforth banned. In an unpublished section of the resolution, provision was made for the expulsion of members of the CC by a two-thirds vote of all members in a joint meeting of the CC and the Party's disciplinary organ, the Central Control Commission.

These resolutions represented a firm rejection of the activities of both the Workers' Opposition and the Democratic Centralists. But the implications of the 'On Party Unity' resolution went much further. A strict reading of this could disallow any form of association or joint action between Party members to criticise the leadership. It is important to recognise, however, that the later destruction of all opposition in the Party did not automatically flow from this resolution. There were numerous provisions in the Party rules that were designed to promote free and open discussion and dissent, and 'On Party Unity' was in principle no more binding on Party members than these other provisions.

But the importance of 'On Party Unity' lay in the fact that it created a weapon which politicians could use in an attempt to stifle dissent.

The defeat of these successive opposition groups was due to three general factors.

Context: On each occasion of opposition, the defeated group favoured a course of action that involved a more radical and less centralised policy or set of arrangements than that proposed by Lenin. This was a time when continued Party rule was under threat; the Civil War, peasant risings, the dissolution of the proletariat and the revolt of the Kronstadt sailors all discouraged risk and experimentation and caused Party members to opt for solutions that would strengthen and consolidate the regime. This sentiment is reflected in a resolution of the Eighth Congress in 1919 which read in part:

'On the Organisational Question', Robert H. McNeal (ed.). *Resolutions and Decisions of the Communist Party of the Soviet Union*, Vol.2, Richard Gregor (ed.), *The Early Soviet Period: 1917–1929*, University of Toronto Press, Toronto, 1974, p.86

> 66 The situation of the party is such that the strictest centralism and the most severe discipline are an absolute necessity. All decisions of higher echelons are absolutely binding for those below. Every resolution must first be carried out, and only then is it permissible to appeal the resolution to the appropriate party body. In this sense regular military discipline is necessary for the party in the present era. All party undertakings susceptible of centralisation (publishing, propaganda etc) must be centralised for effectiveness. 99

Tighter central control seemed more appropriate than the decentralisation the opposition favoured.

Lenin, Trotsky and others in Red Square, Moscow, 1919, celebrating the second anniversary of the October Revolution (Mary Evans/ Alexander Meledin Collection)

The role of Lenin: As the Party's founder and the individual who led it to victory in 1917, Lenin had enormous personal prestige, stature and authority. Although he did not enjoy *unquestioned* authority, many rank-and-file Party members and officials took their lead from Lenin on many issues. Lenin did not get his way on all issues, but whenever he expended major efforts, he was successful. As a figure of authority, Lenin was predominant; a vote by rank-and-file representatives against Lenin in the Party Congress on an important issue was inconceivable.

Organisational manipulation: It is clear that at a number of Congresses during this period, representation was manipulated in such a way as to weaken the position of the opposition and strengthen that of the leadership. Such efforts were probably not crucial in the defeat of these groups; the other two factors were more important. Nevertheless the manipulation of delegate selection that occurred at this time was a foretaste of things to come.

Thus during this period, in very difficult circumstances, the contours of the new regime emerged. Gradually power was becoming centralised in the Party's executive organs, particularly the Politburo. The Congress still played a part in decision-making, but that role was already being eroded by the growth in the power of the Politburo and the organisational manipulation referred to above. This was to become even more marked during the late 1920s.

Discuss

- Discuss the Tenth Congress of the Party and the relationship between the economic policy introduced there and the change in attitude to opposition.

CASE STUDY 3

War Communism: Ideology vs Necessity

PROBLEMS AND ISSUES

- Ideology — in theory and practice

One of the enduring debates in the historiography of the early Soviet period concerns the origins of War Communism. This Case Study will survey this debate. Publications mentioned are listed at the end.

Two basic positions have been put forward regarding the origins of War Communism.

1 War Communism was an ideologically motivated attempt to restructure the society and economy along socialist lines. This interpretation gained currency from the 1920s, when both Leites and Lawton argued that this was a function of Bolshevik doctrine. Lawton even went so far as to argue that 'as fast as they could be committed to paper, all reforms of which the Bolsheviks had dreamt in exile were translated into decrees' (p.78). This position was extended by Paul Craig Roberts, who declared that '(i)t is clear

that the measures of "war communism" were based on an application of Marxian doctrine...' (p.254), and who believed that the policies of War Communism 'were implicit in the doctrine of revolutionary Marxian socialism' (p.245). A Hungarian author, Laszlo Szamuely, argued that while there was no clear ideological program prior to War Communism, the ideas on economic organisation that were dominant in Marxist circles (principally the German Karl Kautsky, but also represented in the work of Nikolai Bukharin) were consistent with the principal elements of War Communism.

Supporters of this view rely upon two main sources to sustain their argument. The first is the general body of pre-1917 Marxist writing, most importantly the work of Marx and Engels themselves. Clearly there are many passages that occur in this body of writing that are consistent with some of the policies that constituted War Communism. The general hostility to private property, the market and commodity relations in the work of Marx, Engels and others provided an obvious foundation upon which the policies of War Communism could rest.

The second, and more important, source to support this argument is the words of Russian leaders themselves at the time. Important here have been a book by Bukharin and his programmatic text written jointly with Preobrazhensky. But more significant have been the words of Lenin. Roberts is a good example of the use of Lenin's words. He cites Lenin from 1917 through to the end of War Communism, showing how during this period Lenin consistently supported the sorts of policies of which War Communism consisted. He reports that at no time did Lenin refer to the policies as temporary or as wartime measures. Furthermore he argues that when Lenin rejects War Communism in favour of the NEP, he does so not by what would appear to be the easy argument, i.e. War Communism was a temporary necessity designed to deal with the wartime conditions, but by saying that the socialist program had been driven to the point of exhaustion by the war. It was not a mistake in principle, but in the wartime conditions it had been pushed too far too fast, and so what was now needed was an economic breathing space.

2 The second position on War Communism saw it as purely a temporary measure, a reaction to the wartime threat with no ideological basis. Probably the most influential statement of this view comes from the authoritative work of Maurice Dobb, who declared that War Communism 'emerges clearly as an empirical creation, not as the *a priori* product of theory: as an improvisation in face of economic scarcity and military urgency in conditions of exhausting civil war' (p.122). This view was also adopted by such leading scholars of the period as R.W. Davies ('The extreme measures of war communism were in essence emergency methods by which the government acquired a maximum share of this reduced output and allocated it to what it regarded as the most essential uses,' p.26) and the doyen of the study of this period, E.H. Carr, although Carr does acknowledge some role for ideology. Bukharin's biographer, Stephen Cohen, also saw War Communism as a 'response to pressing and perilous circumstances' (p.78).

The evidence used by supporters of this second view is mainly circumstantial. They argue that the Bolsheviks did not have any clearly defined program for economic change before they came to power. They argue that the way the individual measures were introduced shows no elaborate foreplanning but responses to immediate problems. They also draw parallels with other states in wartime conditions and point to the similarities.

The issue is, how can this sort of evidence be held to prevail over the words of the chief actor at this time, Lenin?

Consider the Context

The answer to this question lies in context. Lenin's statements regarding War Communism did not occur in a vacuum. Throughout this period, Lenin and his immediate colleagues were under almost continual criticism from the left. One way of blunting this criticism was to define policy in ideological terms. If individual policy measures could be dressed up in ideological garb, regardless of whether they had any ideological roots at all, they would be less likely to stimulate criticism and dissent. For those on the left of the Party who were intent on moving quickly to socialism, the ideological gloss on such policies was more than just gloss; for them, the measures of War Communism may have seemed to be real steps on the road to socialism. In this way, the true believers in rapid socialist transformation could agree with the rhetoric of those who were more concerned with the immediate problems posed by the war, and create a strong ideological underpinning and justification for War Communism.

A similar point of context relates to Lenin's refusal at the time of the introduction of NEP to refer to War Communism as a mistake, or merely a temporary expedient. Given the continuing strength of leftist sentiment in the Party, he could not argue (and at this stage probably did not believe) that NEP could be a new path to socialism. He had to justify it as a temporary setback, a breathing space before the advance could be renewed. He could not justify it in this way if War Communism too had been seen as a temporary measure. Thus it was still in his interests in 1921 to portray War Communism as an ideologically based attempt to move towards socialism.

Evaluating War Communism

How, then, are we to evaluate War Communism? As a recent study of War Communism points out, (Malle) war needs frequently superseded ideological preference, and it was often a culture of militarisation that was more important in determining policy choices than ideological concerns. But even so, when faced with a choice, people usually have a variety of alternatives open to them. Certain alternatives had some consistency with ideological predispositions, and it is likely that these would have been more likely to have been chosen than others. In this sense, War Communism is seen as primarily a response to wartime conditions, but one which was consistent with a certain view of the ideological inheritance which certainly justified and may in part have helped shape the practical lines of policy. The answer is thus neither solely ideology nor necessity, but a response to necessity with an ideological gloss.

List of references

Bukharin, Nikolai, *Economics of the Transformation Period*, Pluto Press, New York, 1971 (originally published 1920).

Bukharin, N. & Preobrazhensky, E., *The ABC of Communism*, Penguin, Harmondsworth, 1969, E.H. Carr (ed.) (originally published 1919).

Carr, E.H., *The Bolshevik Revolution 1917–1923*, Vol.2, Penguin, Harmondsworth, 1966 (originally published 1952).

Cohen, Stephen F., *Bukharin and the Bolshevik Revolution: A Political Biography, 1888–1938*, Oxford University Press, Oxford, 1971.

Davies, R.W., *The Development of the Soviet Budgetary System*, Cambridge University Press, Cambridge, 1958.

Dobb, Maurice, *Soviet Economic Development Since 1917*, Routledge & Kegan Paul, London, 1966 (originally published 1948).

Lawton, L., *An Economic History of Soviet Russia*, Macmillan, London, 1928.

Leites, K., *Recent Economic Development in Russia*, Oxford University Press, Oxford, 1922.

Malle, Silvana, *The Economic Organization of War Communism*, Cambridge University Press, Cambridge, 1985.

Roberts, Paul Craig, '"War Communism": A Re-examination', *Slavic Review* 29, 1970.

Szamuely, Laszlo, *First Models of the Socialist Economic Systems. Principles and theories*, Akademiai Kiado, Budapest, 1974.

Essay Questions

1 What were the main features of the ideology developed by Lenin and the Bolsheviks prior to their seizure of power, and to what extent was it implemented in the period 1918 to 1924?

2 'Commencing as it did about six months after the October Revolution, the Civil War and the severe crisis it produced accounts in large part for Lenin and the Bolsheviks pursuing policies which were often incompatible with those they had been previously advocating.' How valid is this assessment?

3 'Trotsky's creation of the Red Army and the employment of Red Terror, not ideology, were the keys which enabled the Bolsheviks to retain power.' Discuss with reference to the period 1918–20.

4 How and why did the character of the Bolshevik/Communist Party change between 1917 and the Tenth Party Congress in March 1921?

THE GOLDEN TWENTIES

HAVING DEFEATED their external enemies militarily, the Bolsheviks had to face the question of how socialism was best to be achieved in Russia. Here came the clash of ideological principle with the pragmatic demands of survival in a land which was still characterised by considerable hostility to Bolshevik aims and aspirations.

Focus questions

The following questions provide a focus for study in this chapter:

- How was socialism to be achieved according to Lenin?
- Why was there opposition to the NEP in the Party?
- What was the meaning of 'socialism in one country'?
- Why was there significant opposition to Trotsky?

The introduction of the NEP ushered in a period of relaxation and flexibility that Russian society, ravaged by six years of war and revolution, badly needed. This was evident in all spheres of life, but basic to them all was the course of economic development.

THE NEW ECONOMIC POLICY

The central element of the NEP in rural areas was the replacement of forced requisitioning of peasant produce by a tax in kind. Henceforth the peasants paid a set rate of tax and their grain was sold in the marketplace at market prices, thereby providing a level of predictability for producers that had not

Visual displays were used extensively in the struggle against religion. This poster from 1922 by D. Melnikov declares: 'Were the churches' decorations of gold and silver built with kopecks gathered by the peasants so that they could become dark camps? All must be given to the peasants who are dying from hunger' (Sovietsky Khudoznik Publishers, Moscow)

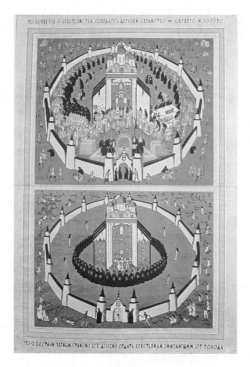

PROBLEMS
AND ISSUES

● Ideology — in
  theory and
  practice

existed under War Communism. The denationalisation of small-scale enterprises, artisans' workshops and craftsmen revived a whole sector of the economy that had been suppressed under War Communism and that was central to the re-emergence of a vigorous market. The revitalisation of market principles was the main factor in the economic revival Russia experienced following the introduction of NEP. Prosperity returned to sections of the countryside, industrial production began to edge closer to its pre-war levels, and the towns and cities again began to grow. By 1926–27 production levels were back to about the level of 1913 (see p.86).

The sort of loosening of central control that was evident in the economy also occurred in other areas of national life. The 'Red Terror' that had been unleashed in the Civil War against presumed class enemies was eliminated as a major element of state policy. The security apparatus (initially called the Cheka, then the GPU and then, in 1924, the OGPU) remained active in the struggle against groups believed to be a threat — former White officers and nobles, religious believers and former members of political parties — but its activities were much more restricted than they had been under War Communism. Indeed, such extra-judicial activity became less important in the context of a 'cult of legality' which emerged at this time. The regeneration of the market created a need for stable bodies of laws to order market relations. During 1922, the government issued separate criminal, civil, agrarian and labour codes. The judicial system was reorganised emphasising a professional judiciary and strict observance of the law. In the middle of the decade, class discrimination, which had been used in an attempt to discriminate positively in favour of the working class, was officially downgraded in the law. A new federal

In the struggle that continued during the NEP, party zealots destroyed many religious artefacts. The Simonov monastery was destroyed in 1927 (Museum of Modern Art, Oxford)

The Revolution and its values challenged many of the customs of the diverse peoples of the old Russian empire. In the Muslim southern parts of the country, it helped the liberation of women. This picture shows a demonstration by women in Tashkent in 1926. They decided to reject the veil they had traditionally been expected to wear. They had to be protected by police from angry men (Museum of Modern Art, Oxford)

constitution was introduced in 1924. All of this helped to create a greater sense of predictability and freedom in public life.

Along with the emphasis upon legality went a decline in the militancy of ideology. Notions of class struggle and the building of socialism were down-played and forms of reconciliation in society were emphasised. The prevailing climate was clearly one of compromise. All social forces, including those deemed to be ideologically tainted like the intelligentsia and the so-called bourgeois experts (technical specialists like engineers who had been trained during the tsarist period) were allowed comparatively free rein. As a result, this period was characterised by substantial intellectual and cultural pluralism and freedom, with widespread public debate occurring on many issues. The Academy of Sciences encouraged vigorous debate, within the framework of Marxist thought, on topics as diverse as law, social theory, historiography and science. Marxism as social theory became much richer as a result of the debates at this time. In society generally, the flourishing of ideas was evident in art, literature, the cinema and the theatre. This was the golden age of twentieth century Russian culture, associated with artists such as Malevich, Rodchenko and Tatlin; writers like Babel, Pasternak, Esenin, Akhmatova, Sholokhov, Zamiatin, Pilnyak, Mayakovsky, Bulgakov, Mandelshtam and Zoshchenko; cinema figures like Eisenstein and Dovzhenko; and Meyerhold in the theatre. The richness of the cultural variety, pluralism and innovation is difficult to exaggerate.

THE DEBATE OVER THE NEP

PROBLEMS AND ISSUES

● Ideology — in theory and practice

When the NEP was introduced at the Tenth Congress in 1921, it was accepted as a temporary retreat. War Communism was portrayed as an attempt to move toward socialism that had been blocked by the strength of opposition. What was needed, Lenin told the delegates, was a breathing space, a means of drawing back from the struggle to enable the Party to gather its strength before once again embarking on the task of socialist construction. The fact that international revolution was not imminent meant that the Party had to rely on its own efforts to safeguard the revolution in Russia. This aim could only be achieved, according to Lenin, by a compromise with the hostile forces inside the country. The NEP was to be this temporary compromise, a short-term arrangement to enable the Party to gather strength for the final assault.

The Organisation of Co-operatives

Towards the end of his life, however, Lenin's view of the NEP changed. Instead of being a short-term compromise, he began to see it as a viable means of reaching socialism both in Russia and abroad. For Lenin, the key to the attainment of socialism was the organisation of co-operatives. In one of his last articles, written in January 1923, he declared:

> All we actually need under NEP is to organise the population of Russia in co-operative societies on a sufficiently large scale, for we have now found that degree of combination of private interest, of private commercial interest, with state supervision and control of this interest, that degree of its subordination to the common interests which was formerly the stumbling block for very many socialists. Indeed, the power of the state over all large-scale

In the mid-1920s, the party followed a policy of seeking to establish a smychka (alliance or union) between the proletariat and the peasantry. This 1925 poster by B. Kustodiev and distributed by the Leningrad Society for the Alliance of Town and Village declares: 'To establish contacts between town and village is one of the most important tasks of the working class in power' (Sovietsky Khudoznik Publishers, Moscow)

ЛЕНИНГРАДСКОЕ ОБЩЕСТВО
СМЫЧКИ ГОРОДА С ДЕРЕВНЕЙ.

Установить общение между городом и деревней, одна из основных задач рабочего класса, стоящего у власти. В. И. ЛЕНИН.

'On Co-operation', Lenin, *Collected Works*, Vol.33, p.468

means of production, political power in the hands of the proletariat, the alliance of this proletariat with the many millions of small and very small peasants, the assured proletarian leadership of the peasantry, etc. — is this not all that is necessary to build a complete socialist society out of co-operatives, out of co-operatives alone, which we formerly ridiculed as hucks-tering and which from a certain aspect we have the right to treat as such now, under NEP? Is this not all that is necessary to build a complete socialist society? It is still not the building of socialist society, but it is all that is necessary and sufficient for it. **"**

Lenin saw the growth of the co-operative movement as virtually identical with the growth of socialism, a development that was to take place within the socio-economic framework of the NEP. This required the gaining of higher levels of culture, defined principally in terms of education and literacy, before social-ism could be achieved and would take 'a whole historical epoch'. The NEP was to be a 'long series of gradual transformations into a large-scale socialised economy'. Although Lenin's views, as spelled out in his last articles, remain incomplete, it is clear that he envisaged the maintenance of the NEP social order — based on proletarian–peasant collaboration — as essential to the move toward socialism. This stance was to be the basis for Bukharin's opposition to Stalin later in the decade.

Opposition to NEP

There had been a core of opposition to the NEP in the Party from the time it had been introduced. It was a clear concession to capitalist forces in the countryside. In the minds of many Party members this concession sat uneasily with the anti-capitalist sentiments that had driven the October Revolution. Such opposition gathered strength, momentum and voice in 1923 with the first 'scissors crisis'*; agricultural prices fell while industrial prices rose, thereby eliminating the incentive for grain producers to market their grain. Although this price divergence narrowed in 1924, the lesson was clear to the critics of the NEP: reliance on market forces left the towns and the regime dependent on the peasant producers who, in ideological terms, were considered an unreliable and reluctant ally. This opposition grew stronger in 1926–27.

Central to the debate over the NEP was its capacity to sustain a high level of industrial development. Initially industrial development was largely the result of the reactivation of industry that had fallen into disuse during the period of war, revolution and civil war. By the middle of the decade, however, expansion on this basis had reached its limit. In the absence of investment, industrial development slowed. So too did agricultural production, as Table 4.1 shows.

Roger A. Clarke & Dubravko J.I. Matko, *Soviet Economic Facts 1917–81*, London, Macmillan, 1983, pp.10 & 13

PROBLEMS AND ISSUES

- Ideology — in theory and practice
- Modernisation

Table 4.1 Economic Development Under the NEP

	Industrial Production		Agricultural Production	
	Index	Percentage increase over previous year	Index	Percentage increase over previous year
1913	100		100	
1921	31		60	
1924	45		90	
1925	73	62.2	112	24.4
1926	98	34.2	118	5.4
1927	111	13.3	121	2.5
1928	132	18.9	124	2.5

This slowdown in economic growth coincided with strengthening demands for increased levels of industrial development. There were three immediate reasons for these demands.

Communism equals abundance: The general ideological association of communism with material plenty. This of necessity presupposed industrialisation. If industrialisation was an essential part of the construction of socialism, progress towards this aim demanded positive industrial achievements. With

---

* The term 'scissors crisis' comes from a graph devised by Trotsky showing rising industrial prices and falling agricultural prices. The two axes of the graph looked like the widening blades of a pair of scissors.

The growing pressures for industrialisation are reflected in this poster by P. Shukhmin celebrating the tenth anniversary of the Revolution. The text reads: 'Under the banner of the VKP (b) (the communist party) we are marching to socialism along the path of Lenin' (Sovietsky Khudoznik Publishers, Moscow)

the slackening of growth, the ultimate aim seemed to be cast into doubt. What was immediately evident about this was the decline in enthusiasm and commitment among many Party members during this period. The excitement and sense of achievement that had accompanied victory in October and the Civil War had given way to the humdrum life of administration, and many of those radical, activist workers who had flocked into the Party were becoming disillusioned. A sense of the building of socialism needed to be maintained.

A sense of domestic insecurity: This consisted of the view that the 'proletarian dictatorship' was insecure in the overwhelmingly petit bourgeois peasant environment of Russia. Party meetings and documents from this period frequently reflect the fear that the regime was degenerating as a result of infection from the petit bourgeois environment. This sort of fear grew from the belief that the Party and the regime could be swamped by the peasantry, a class with interests and priorities antagonistic to those of the proletariat, which the Party represented. A consequent loss of the Party's proletarian essence was feared. This fear explains the discrimination in favour of workers in the Party's recruitment policies during this period.

More immediately, this insecurity rested on the Party's need to rely on the class enemy both for its survival and for progress towards its ultimate aim, socialism. The market mechanism of the NEP made the regime totally reliant upon the willingness of the peasants to respond to market forces and to provide the produce necessary both to feed the cities and to finance future development. In addition, the small number of technical specialists in industry trained since

1917 meant that reliance upon those trained under the tsar, the 'bourgeois specialists', was necessary. In the eyes of many in the Party, these were a suspect group — the class enemy whose training, background and interests were opposed to those of the Bolsheviks. Concern about the power of this group is reflected in Lenin's speech to the Eleventh Congress in 1922:

> And here we must squarely put the question: wherein lies our strength and what do we lack? We have quite enough political power. I hardly think there is anyone here who will assert that on such-and-such a practical question, in such-and-such a business institution, the Communists, the Communist Party, lack sufficient power… What then is lacking? Obviously, what is lacking is culture among the stratum of the Communists who perform administrative functions. If we take Moscow with its 4700 Communists in responsible positions, and if we take that huge bureaucratic machine, that gigantic heap, we must ask: who is directing whom? I doubt very much whether it can truthfully be said that the Communists are directing that heap. To tell the truth, they are not directing, they are being directed. Something analogous happened here to what we were told in our history lessons when we were children: sometimes one nation conquers another, the nation that conquers is the conqueror and the nation that is vanquished is the conquered nation. This is simple and intelligible to all. But what happens to the culture of these nations? Here things are not so simple. If the conquering nation is more cultivated than the vanquished nation, the former imposes its culture upon the latter; but if the opposite is the case, the vanquished nation imposes its culture upon the conqueror. Has not something like this happened in the capital of the RSFSR. Have the 4700 Communists (nearly a whole army division, and all of them the very best) come under the influence of an alien culture? True, there may be the impression that the vanquished have a high level of culture. But that is not the case at all. Their culture is miserable, insignificant, but it is still at a higher level than ours. Miserable and low as it is, it is higher than that of our responsible Communist administrators, for the latter lack administrative ability. Communists who are put at the head of departments — and sometimes artful saboteurs deliberately put them in these positions in order to use them as a shield — are often fooled.

'Political Report of the Central Committee of the RCP(b), March 27', Lenin, *Collected Works*, Vol.33, pp.287–8

In the face of these domestic challenges, the regime had to build up the power of the proletariat. This could be achieved only through industrialisation.

An important practical aspect of this domestic sense of insecurity stemming from the petit bourgeois environment was the Party's weakness in rural areas. Throughout this period the Party was unable to penetrate rural society effectively. According to Party records, in 1924 in one area of 50 000 to 60 000 villages, there were only ten communists. Four years later there were only 20 660 rural Party cells to cover 546 747 population centres in the countryside; only 0.7 per cent of peasant households included a Party member. Without secure roots in the countryside, the Party had little control outside the cities.

A sense of international insecurity: Foreign intervention in the Civil War, the hostile statements of Western political leaders, and trade embargoes on the Soviet Union demonstrated the unsympathetic international

PROBLEMS
AND ISSUES

● Ideology — in
  theory
● Counter-revolution
● Modernisation

environment within which the new state had to survive. Following the abortive German uprising of 1923 (the event which finally brought home to many that international revolution was still a long way off), the external environment seemed to improve, at least temporarily. Cordial relations had existed with Germany since 1922, and in 1924 Britain, Italy and France formally recognised the USSR. But recognition did not mean friendship. Through the Treaty of Locarno signed at the end of 1925, the Western powers attempted to wean Germany away from her Soviet connection and to isolate the 'Bolshevik menace'. Although not completely successful, their efforts did see some weakening of the Soviet–German link.

Relations between the USSR and the capitalist powers were correct rather than friendly and always rested on a shaky basis. This was ably demonstrated by the way in which the British government broke off relations with the USSR in May 1927 for purely domestic political reasons. This was immediately followed by a war scare in the USSR, stemming from the belief that foreign powers were about to attack. In the absence of world revolution (an event made even more unlikely by the Communist failure in China in 1927) and confronted by a hostile environment, the connection between defence and increased levels of industrialisation was inescapable. If the Revolution and the new Soviet state were to be defended, higher levels of industrialisation were essential.

Discuss

- For what reasons did the Bolsheviks look to revolution in the West? How did the failed uprisings in Germany in 1923 and China in 1927 affect internal Bolshevik policies?

- Why did the arts and sciences flourish in this period? Can you think of comparable periods in history?

ALTERNATIVE PATHS TO INDUSTRIALISATION

PROBLEMS
AND ISSUES

● Ideology — in
  theory
● Modernisation

By 1927, most of the Party agreed on the need to increase the tempo of industrialisation. The left in the Party had favoured this from the beginning of the NEP while the right too had come to accept it. But industrialisation had to be financed principally from Russia's own resources. Significant levels of aid and assistance were not forthcoming from the capitalist world, which was reluctant to invest in a country that had repudiated tsarist government debts after the October Revolution. The capital for industrialisation had, therefore, to come from the peasants. But the state faced a problem: it needed to maximise the peasants' *off-farm surplus* (the difference between what the peasant produced and consumed). This surplus would then increase grain exports and provide income to pay for imports of machinery and to finance development projects. One way of increasing off-farm surplus would have been to offer high prices for grain to encourage the peasants to produce and sell more. But the lower the purchase price, the more capital was freed for investment in industrial development. Here was the basic point at issue in the economic debates of the 1920s: how to maximise the rural contribution to industrialisation.

Co-operation and Gradual Development...

Two types of answer were suggested to this problem. The first was associated with Bukharin and the right, and took its lead from Lenin's last articles and his positive evaluation of the NEP. The basis of this view was the belief that the move into socialism should proceed at the pace the peasantry was willing to accept. This rested on a notion of balanced, or 'organic', development: the continued operation of the market would lead to the gradual improvement of agriculture, resulting in higher surpluses that could be ploughed into industry. The peasant was to 'grow into socialism'. This strategy required an increase in production of consumer goods to provide incentives for the peasants to produce and market their grain. Although by 1926 Bukharin accepted that capital accumulation had to take place at the expense of the peasants, he was still convinced that co-operation with them was essential for the achievement of the regime's goals.

An early Russian tractor. Russian agricultural methods were extremely backward, and tractors such as this were introduced slowly (SCR)

There were three problems with this strategy:

- This course of development would have been slow, and was thus out of step with the growing air of urgency that was taking hold in the Party.
- This would have demanded the outlay of substantial resources on either the production or import of consumer goods. But if the basic aim was to increase the production of heavy industry, the redirection of resources into the production of consumer goods seemed to be counter-productive.
- Reliance on agricultural improvement to stimulate industrial development would have strengthened the position of the *kulaks*, or rich peasants. Generally these were the more efficient producers and the ones who could make the best use of the market. This sort of strategy would therefore have assisted and strengthened the class enemies.

... or Increased State Control

In opposition to the strategy put forward by the right was one championed by the left. Originally this was associated with Trotsky and Evgenii Preobrazhensky, but from late spring 1928 Stalin was also a supporter. The basic position adopted by the left was that the required accumulation of capital could not be achieved through voluntary savings; it had to be 'pumped' from the private sector of the economy. The easiest method of doing this was through taxation, but Preobrazhensky also called for the direct exploitation of the private sector. This meant that the state should use its position of control over the supply of most industrial goods and its monopoly of foreign trade to structure the terms of trade between city and countryside, so as to exploit the latter and obtain the necessary resources. In this view, the state should depress the prices of agricultural produce and raise those of industrial and consumer goods in order to maximise the flow of resources from the countryside. The widespread use of armed requisitioning and the forced collectivisation of agriculture were not seen as part of the answer until 1928–29.

At the Fourteenth Congress of the Party in December 1925, a resolution placing increased emphasis on industrialisation was adopted. At the Fifteenth Congress two years later, resolutions were adopted calling for voluntary agricultural collectivisation and the drafting of a five-year-plan for economic development. At this stage there was no sign of the radical transformation that was to come: targets remained moderate, and collectivisation was to be voluntary. The grain procurement crisis in late 1927 and early 1928 changed Party perceptions. A revival of the scissors crisis led to grain shortages and to the charge that the *kulaks* were holding the state to ransom. Many complained that the *kulaks* were refusing to sell their grain in the hope either of forcing up the price or of driving the government from office. Ignoring calls from the right to solve this problem by increasing grain prices, Stalin and his supporters resorted to what came to be known as the 'Urals–Siberian method': the requisitioning of grain by armed force. By the middle of 1928, such measures had been abandoned, at least temporarily. The Party leadership remained publicly united, although this unity was little more than a facade.

There is no evidence that conclusively proves when Stalin became finally committed to the full-scale collectivisation of agriculture that began in late 1929. By April 1929 Stalin was convinced of the need to eliminate private agriculture, but he may not have come to accept forced collectivisation until the northern autumn of 1929, by which time the right was well and truly defeated. Certainly plan targets were increased to unrealistic levels at the Sixteenth Congress in April 1929 (industrial output was to increase by 180 per cent, investment by 228 per cent, consumption by nearly 70 per cent and agricultural output by 55 per cent), but this did not constitute the effective declaration of war against the peasantry that collectivisation was to become.

Discuss

- Compare the political symbolism contained in the posters on pp.85, 87 and 93. What does this tell us about the class basis of the regime?

Review

- What would the political consequences have been of the adoption of opposition economic policies in the 1920s?

SHAKHTY AND THE SPECIALISTS

PROBLEMS AND ISSUES
- Ideology — in theory and practice
- Counter-revolution

Agricultural collectivisation was seen as the solution to the dilemma posed by the petit bourgeois countryside and economy. Its methods and success will be discussed in the following chapter. But Party leaders also felt threatened by the place and role of the bourgeois experts. A move against them too was initiated towards the end of the 1920s. In March 1928 the Shakhty trial was announced. A group of engineers from the Shakhty region of the Donbas was accused of deliberate sabotage in the mining industry and of being in league with foreign powers. This trial was followed by trials of bourgeois experts in other parts of the economy. The main theme of the trials was the link between the domestic class enemy and hostile capitalist powers. Their effect was to cast suspicion over all the technical experts working in the Soviet economy, undermining the position their expertise gave them by questioning their loyalty, and subjecting them to harassment and intimidation.

These sorts of attacks on the specialists had two significant effects. The first was a positive effect: it provided the stimulus for the large-scale mobilisation of working-class youth into the expanding educational facilities to gain technical knowledge and expertise. Trained under the Soviet regime, they were not under suspicion in the way that those experts trained in pre-revolutionary times were. These newly trained specialists became an important social basis for the regime in the coming years.

The second effect was that it hardened Party opinion against the peasantry. The campaign against the specialists highlighted the vulnerability of the regime to petit bourgeois forces, of which the peasants were the most powerful. The turn to agricultural collectivisation was linked with the anti-bourgeois specialist ethos at the end of the decade.

Discuss

- If you had been a working-class delegate to the Fourteenth Congress of the Communist Party, what would have been your evaluation of the debate over the development of industry?
- What would your opinion of the Shakhty trials have been?

POWER AND AUTHORITY IN THE PARTY

The course of socio-economic development throughout the 1920s culminating in the 'great transformation' was a crucial influence on the Communist Party during this period. Lenin suffered a stroke in May 1922 and although he returned to work briefly in October, another stroke rendered him unfit for regular work in mid-December 1922. A third stroke in March 1923 was totally disabling. His last letters and article were dictated to his secretaries in short sessions over a period of days in December 1922 and January 1923. They contained his positive re-evaluation of NEP noted above. Lenin died on 21 January 1924.

Poster by A. Strakhov dating from 1924. It commemorates Vladimir Lenin, founder of the Soviet state, who died that year (Sovietsky Khudoznik Publishers, Moscow)

There was no logical successor to Lenin. His predominant position in the Party and regime was due to his personal role in the Party's history and its rise to power rather than to his occupation of any particular office in the political structure. Indeed, apart from membership of the CC and Politburo, Lenin did not occupy a Party office; his sole official position was chairman of *Sovnarkom*, or prime minister. Furthermore, officially leadership was collective, vested in collective Party organs, so there was no leadership position for any successor to Lenin to fill in the hope of replacing the dead leader. The power struggle that followed Lenin's illness broke into the open just prior to his death. The crucial factor in this struggle was the ability to secure support in the leading organs of the Party. In retrospect, Stalin was the best placed organisationally and the most skilful actor politically of those who sought the dead leader's mantle.

The General Secretary

PROBLEMS AND ISSUES

● Role of the party

The basis of Stalin's organisational power was the position of Party general secretary, to which he was appointed in April 1922. Following the death of the first party secretary Yakov Sverdlov in March 1919, the Orgburo and Secretariat were established, but there had been general dissatisfaction with the way these bodies had functioned. The post of general secretary was meant to remedy this, and Stalin was appointed to it because it was felt that his skills lay in the organisational arena, not in public political matters. But instead of this position being one of little power, as most had assumed it would be,

Lenin and Stalin in 1922. This photograph, taken while Lenin was ill, was used by Stalin during the 1920s to demonstrate the closeness between the two leaders (Warder Collection)

The temporary wooden mausoleum built in 1924 to take Lenin's body. It was later replaced by a marble structure (BBC Hulton Picture Library, London)

it proved to be crucial to the internal operation of the Party. The key to this was the structural location of the post.

The three executive organs created in 1919 — the Politburo, Orgburo and Secretariat — were interlocking bodies with some membership overlap. From his appointment as general secretary, Stalin was the only full (voting) member of all three bodies. This provided him with significant potential for manipulation. Membership of the Politburo gave access to supreme decision-making circles. Membership of the Orgburo gave access to the power to direct personnel to carry out Politburo decisions and to fill vacancies in the Party hierarchy. Leadership of the Secretariat gave some control over the flow of information to the Politburo and the setting of its agendas. The Secretariat also gave further access to the machinery of directing personnel, which the Secretariat carried out under the authority of the Orgburo. The main organisational threads of the Party thus came together in the hands of the general secretary. This gave Stalin considerable power and was an important factor in determining the outcome of the elite conflicts that wracked the Party following Lenin's death (see Case Study 4).

Review

- Put yourself in the position of the editor of *Pravda*: write an editorial for your newspaper for May 1928 in which you explain the Shakhty trial.

THE STRUGGLE WITH TROTSKY

Before Lenin's death, groups and individuals began to manoeuvre to gain the advantage in the succession struggle that all knew was coming. Initially, most manoeuvring was directed against Trotsky. Although considered by some (including Lenin) the most able member of the leadership, Trotsky was widely disliked in leadership circles. His late entry to the party (he joined in August 1917) and his history of bitter disputes with Lenin before the revolution made many see him as a 'johnny come lately'. These opponents were critical because Trotsky had not earned his leading position in the party through a long apprenticeship but had come to it at the last minute when success was in sight. His imperious ways and authoritarian style of leadership, reinforced by a certain personal insensitivity, alienated many from him. But as well as personal dislike and jealousy, there were other fears in the minds of some leaders. Considering parallels from French revolutionary history, many saw Trotsky's position as war commissar as a potential threat of 'Bonapartism' or a military coup. As a result of these fears and resentments, the so-called troika was formed between Stalin, Zinoviev and Kamenev in 1923.

> **PROBLEMS AND ISSUES**
> - Role of the party and state

The simmering hostility burst into the open in late 1923 with a letter from Trotsky to the CC. In this he roundly criticised government economic policy and the unhealthy practice of filling key posts in the Party apparatus by appointment rather than election. The letter called for the democratisation of the Party and the elimination of the psychology whereby it was believed 'that the secretarial hierarchy [i.e. full-time Party officials] is the proper apparatus for forming Party opinions and making Party decisions' (Leon Trotsky, *The Challenge of the Left Opposition 1923–25*, Naomi Allen (ed.), New York, Pathfinder Press, 1975, p.56). This letter, backed by criticisms contained in the so-called 'Platform of the 46' that appeared a few days later, was a direct attack on the Party's central secretarial apparatus. This apparatus, through Stalin who as general secretary was its head, supported the troika. At the end of 1923 the troika responded with a full-scale public attack on Trotsky.

Socialism in One Country

The public debate contained a large measure of personal vilification of Trotsky who, because of a mysterious medical condition that incapacitated him at various times, was unable effectively to combat these personal attacks. But the debate also produced an important development in the ideological sphere, the doctrine of 'socialism in one country'. Until autumn 1924 the orthodox position was that although the proletariat could take power in a single country, it could not achieve the final victory of socialism without revolution in several advanced countries. Stalin now argued that Russia could build socialism fully without having to rely on the international proletariat; socialism could be

> **PROBLEMS AND ISSUES**
> - Ideology — in theory and practice

built in one country regardless of the fate of the international revolution. The achievement of socialism was thus presented as being no longer dependent upon events outside Russia's borders. This contrasted sharply with the view that world revolution was necessary for Russia to achieve socialism, a position with which Trotsky was closely associated.

While the introduction of socialism in one country had no immediate implications for Soviet domestic or foreign policy, it was important in terms of the power struggle. It helped the troika present themselves as people with confidence in the capacities of the Russian proletariat, and to present Trotsky as relying on non-Russian forces for success in Russia. A message that promised to successfully build socialism in Russia was likely to be more attractive to people in the Party than Trotsky's message of reliance on the world proletariat. By emphasising Trotsky's lack of faith in the Russian proletariat and his conflicts with the dead Lenin, and through the skilful manipulation of personnel, the troika was able to discredit Trotsky. On 17 January 1925 he was removed as war commissar, and although he retained his Politburo membership, he was politically a spent force.

THE LEFT OPPOSITION

The basis of unity of the troika was always weak, resting on shared opposition to Trotsky. Once Trotsky had ceased to be a threat, the alliance disintegrated. The split among the former members of the troika developed during 1925. It became public in the autumn when Zinoviev openly reversed his former stand of supporting concessions to the peasantry and vigorously criticised this policy. Zinoviev also published a book at this time entitled *Leninism: An Introduction to the Study of Leninism* in which, among other things, he emphasised the internationalist dimension of Leninism and of the revolution. This was a direct attack upon the main supporter of the NEP, Bukharin, and on the originator of the new doctrine of socialism in one country, Stalin.

PROBLEMS AND ISSUES

● Role of the party

The debate continued at the Fourteenth Congress of the Party in December 1925. But here the process of selection of delegates to the Congress was crucial. Although Zinoviev ensured that the delegation from Leningrad, where he was party chief, consisted of his supporters, Stalin and his supporters dominated the other delegations. As a result, the resolution supporting the official policy sponsored by Stalin was adopted by 559 votes to 65. The defeat of the Left Opposition at the Congress led to the removal of its leaders from their positions. Zinoviev remained a full member of the Politburo until July 1926 (and president of the Communist International; he was removed from his leading position in Leningrad). Kamenev remained a candidate member of the Politburo until October 1926. But both were effectively powerless from early 1926.

THE UNITED OPPOSITION

At the Fourteenth Congress, Zinoviev had called for the re-entry into active Party work of all former oppositionists, hinting at the same time that they should combine to oppose Stalin. This call was partly realised in the spring and summer of 1926 with the emergence of the United Opposition, a group which included former foes Zinoviev, Kamenev and Trotsky. The presence of the already rejected Trotsky posed a problem for the United Opposition. A resolution of the Fifteenth Conference of the Party in late 1926 ably illustrates this:

> The party proceeds from the fact that our revolution is a socialist revolution, that the October Revolution is not only a signal, a stimulus, and a point of departure for a socialist revolution in the West, but is at the same time, first, a basis for the subsequent development of world revolution and, second, the opening of the transitional period from capitalism to socialism in the USSR (the dictatorship of the proletariat), during the course of which the proletariat — given a correct policy regarding the peasantry — can and will successfully build a complete socialist society, if, of course, the power of the international revolutionary movement on the one hand and the power of the proletariat of the USSR on the other, will be great enough in order to guard the USSR from the military intervention of imperialism.
>
> Trotskyism adheres to completely different views on the character and perspectives of our revolution. Despite the fact that trotskyism went along with the party in October 1917, it proceeded and continues to proceed from the point that our revolution *in itself* is not, *in essence*, socialist; that the October Revolution is *only* a signal, a stimulus, and a point of departure for a socialist revolution in the West; that if delay ensues in the world revolution and the victorious socialist revolution in the West does not come very soon, the proletarian power in Russia must collapse or degenerate (which is one and the same) under the pressure of unavoidable clashes between the proletariat and the peasantry.
>
> While the party, in organising the October Revolution, proceeded from the fact that 'the victory of socialism is possible originally in a few or even in one capitalist country taken separately'; that 'the victorious pro-letariat of this country, having expropriated the capitalists and having organised its socialist production', can and must stand up '*against* the rest of the capitalist world by attracting to itself the oppressed classes of other countries by encouraging them to rise up against the capitalists, if necessary by coming out even with armed might against the exploiting classes and their states' (Lenin). Trotskyism, on the contrary, collaborating with the Bolsheviks in the October period, proceeded from the view that 'it is hopeless to think ... that, for example, revolutionary Russia could stand its ground in the face of conservative Europe' (Trotsky)...
>
> The conference asserts that the views of Comrade Trotsky and those of one mind with him on the fundamental question of the character and perspectives of our revolution have nothing in common with the views of our party, with leninism...

The basic fact in the development of intra-party relations in the AUCP [All-Union Communist Party] after the XIV Congress (which discussed the principal views of the 'new opposition') is the circumstance that the 'new opposition' (comrades Zinoviev, Kamenev) which earlier fought against trotskyism, against social democratic deviation in our party, went over to the side of the ideological position of trotskyism; that it wholly and fully gave up its former all-party positions for trotskyism and now comes out *for* with the same fervour with which it came out *against* trotskyism before. **"**

'On the Opposition Bloc in the AUCP(b)', 3 November 1926, *Resolutions and Decisions of the Communist Party,* Vol.2, pp.292–4

The United Opposition was easily ridiculed and discredited by the combination of these former enemies.

Furthermore the group had no clearly defined policy positions other than a denunciation of the existing power structure within the Party. Their criticisms led to the expulsion of Trotsky and Kamenev from the Politburo in October 1926, threats to expel them from the Party, and a crescendo of attacks on them in the press. The issue was resolved in the autumn of 1927 when the leaders of the United Opposition mounted their own organised public demonstrations in honour of the tenth anniversary of the Revolution. These were

During the leadership struggles of the 1920s the creative rewriting of history was an important weapon. At the top is the original picture of Lenin addressing a crowd in Sverdlov Square on 5 May 1920. Beside him are Trotsky and Kamenev. Below is the same picture retouched by Stalin (Mansell Collection)

officially described as hostile demonstrations. The leaders of the United Opposition had taken the intra-party struggle into the streets. Supported by Bukharin and the right, Stalin had Trotsky and Zinoviev expelled from the Party in November; Kamenev was expelled from the CC and, in December, from the Party. Trotsky was sent into internal exile in Alma Ata (in Kazakhstan), and a year later began his trip into foreign exile, which was to end in Mexico. Zinoviev and Kamenev, who were readmitted to the Party the following year, were sent to Kaluga, 130 kilometres from Moscow. Many of their rank-and-file supporters were also expelled from the Party.

THE RIGHT OPPOSITION

PROBLEMS AND ISSUES

● Role of the party

With the defeat of the United Opposition and Stalin's use of forceful measures of grain collection in January–February 1928, differences began to surface between Stalin and his erstwhile colleagues on the right. The right, led by Bukharin, Alexei Rykov and Mikhail Tomsky, condemned the effects of the policy of rapid industrialisation and of Stalin's use of force against the peasants. But such criticisms remained private, expressed within the closed meetings of the Politburo and CC rather than through the press. The conflict continued throughout 1928 and 1929, always behind closed doors, and always with the right being steadily undermined. By late 1929, Stalin and his supporters felt sufficiently strong to launch a campaign of denunciation in the press. The opposition signed a formal recantation of their views that was published in the party newspaper *Pravda*, and the CC removed Bukharin from the Politburo and censured Rykov and Tomsky. The last opposition group with the potential to generate support at lower levels of the Party had failed. Stalin remained, apparently supreme.

Discuss

● Discuss this proposition: To view Marxism simply as a rigid set of ideas, as a definitive economic interpretation of history formulated by the German philosopher, Karl Marx, during the mid- to late-nineteenth century and without need of change, is to fail to appreciate the true nature and strength of the ideology to which Marx gave rise. The debates within the Russian Communist Party, especially during the 1920s, illustrate very effectively the crucial characteristic of Marxist ideology: that it is an ever growing, expanding set of ideas capable of adaptation and modification and of adjustment to meet the requirements of changed circumstances.

● Compare the political resources possessed by Stalin and his opponents. Why did Stalin always win?

Stalin's Rise to Personal Power in the 1920s

The failure of the successive opposition groups in the 1920s was an important aspect of the consolidation of Stalin's power. An analysis of the factors behind his rise to power will help to explain the reasons for the failure of those groups.

Stalin's rise to the top of the political ladder had to overcome a large obstacle right from the outset: the negative opinion of him that was Lenin's legacy to the party. While Lenin had approved of Stalin's appointment as Commissar of Nationalities (26 October 1917), of State Control (9 April 1919) and of Workers' and Peasants' Inspection (7 February 1920), his membership of the Politburo and his appointment as general secretary in April 1922, by the time of his death, he had called for Stalin's removal. In a document officially called 'Letter to the Congress' but usually referred to as Lenin's 'Testament' and written in December 1922, Lenin declared:

> Comrade Stalin, having becoming General Secretary, has concentrated unlimited power in his hands, and I am not sure whether he will always be capable of using that authority with sufficient caution. Comrade Trotsky, on the other hand, as his struggle against the CC on the question of the People's Commissariat for Communications has already proved, is distinguished not only by outstanding ability. He is personally perhaps the most capable man in the present CC, but he has displayed excessive self-assurance and shown excessive preoccupation with the purely administrative side of the work.
>
> These two qualities of the two outstanding leaders of the present CC can inadvertently lead to a split, and if our Party does not take steps to avert this, the split may come unexpectedly.
>
> I shall not give any further appraisals of the personal qualities of other members of the CC. I shall just recall that the October episode with Zinoviev and Kamenev was, of course, no accident, but neither can the blame for it be laid upon them personally, any more than non-Bolshevism can upon Trotsky.
>
> Speaking of the young CC members, I wish to say a few words about Bukharin and Pyatakov. They are, in my opinion, the most outstanding figures (among the youngest ones), and the following must be borne in mind about them: Bukharin is not only a most valuable and major theorist of the Party; he is also rightly considered the favourite of the whole Party, but his theoretical views can be classified fully Marxist only with great reserve, for there is something scholastic about him (he has never made a study of dialectics, and, I think, never fully understood it).
>
> ... As for Pyatakov, he is unquestionably a man of outstanding will and outstanding ability, but shows too much zeal for administering and the administrative side of the work to be relied upon in a serious political matter.

Lenin, *Collected Works*, Vol.36, pp.494–6

Having characterised his colleagues in this none too flattering fashion, some days later Lenin added a paragraph to the letter:

> 66 Stalin is too rude, and this defect, fully tolerable in our midst and in dealings among us communists, becomes intolerable in the office of General Secretary. Therefore I propose to the comrades that they devise a way to remove Stalin from this post and appoint to this post another man who differs from comrade Stalin only in one weighty respect, namely in being more tolerant, more loyal, more polite and more attentive to comrades, less capricious etc. 99

Lenin, *Collected Works*, Vol.36, pp.494–6

Lenin's judgment of his comrades and his call for the removal of Stalin remained a secret in the party until the time of the Thirteenth Congress in May 1924. At the Congress, the letter was read to representatives of the different Party delegations in a closed meeting. This was very dangerous for Stalin because of the call for his removal. However Zinoviev and Kamenev, currently in alliance with Stalin against Trotsky, were able to neutralise the effect of the letter. Lenin's opinion was declared to be mistaken, and accordingly could not be used as a weapon against Stalin.

Stalin's organisational placement gave him power that he could use to consolidate his position. Being the point at which the Politburo, Orgburo and Secretariat overlapped, Stalin was uniquely placed to filter the passage of business to the Politburo and to influence the filling of responsible positions at all levels of the political apparatus. The former power may have been less effective than it appears because during this period the other members of the Politburo were all important party personages in their own right with their own channels of communication to the lower levels of the Party. They could all raise any matters for discussion that they believed ought to be raised. But it is the other power, that over personnel distribution, that has usually been seen as the most important factor in Stalin's rise.

From the beginning of Bolshevik rule, appointment was more important than election as a means of filling Party posts. The Orgburo and Secretariat had wide-ranging powers to make many appointments themselves, while lower level bodies had to be supervised in this regard by these central organs. This meant that Stalin was able, through his leadership of the Orgburo and Secretariat, to ensure the appointment of supporters to positions of responsibility throughout the political structure. Even when positions were not filled by established supporters of Stalin, the person appointed may have developed some sense of gratitude and obligation to Stalin for the latter's role in his promotion. Stalin used this power to good end. By supervising the filling of positions in the regional Party apparatus, Stalin was able to consolidate his position at the top of the Party structure. By ensuring that supporters dominated in the regional Party apparatus and that those people were in charge of delegate selection for the Party Congress, Stalin was able to make the Congress a pliable and supportive assembly. It was this process that was at the heart of the heckling and vilification of opposition speakers at Party Congresses from the Thirteenth Congress on. But it should not be assumed that people thus appointed were mere instruments of Stalin. They retained some autonomy, with the result that Stalin had to reinforce the support based on patronage by other means.

PROBLEMS AND ISSUES

● Role of the party

The Cult of Lenin

One method of doing this was to cloak himself in the mantle of authority of Lenin. With the removal of Lenin from active political life, a cult of the leader was developed. This was boosted by his death, with the emergence of such physical symbols of the dead leader as the collection of all of his written works and their publication in a single series of volumes, the placing of his embalmed body in a mausoleum in Red Square, the renaming of the city of Petrograd as Leningrad, the construction of monuments to him in the main cities of the USSR, and the declaration of 21 January as a day of national mourning. There was a growing tendency by all who aspired to high Party office to wrap themselves in Leninist garb. They continually invoked the dead leader's name and cited his writings in support of the particular policy line they were currently supporting. The person who was perceived as the best Leninist, the truest to Lenin's thinking and writing, would be the one best placed to inherit Lenin's authority. Initially Trotsky, Zinoviev and Stalin sought to do this, but there was a clear difference in the image they projected. Both Trotsky and Zinoviev portrayed themselves as Lenin's colleagues and equals, a picture that did not sit easily with the growing air of veneration around the founder of the Soviet state. In contrast, Stalin projected himself as Lenin's disciple, presenting Lenin's works in a simplified, even catechismic, style. This is demonstrated by Stalin's funeral oration for Lenin:

> Leaving us, comrade Lenin enjoined us to hold high and keep pure the great calling of member of the party. We vow to thee, comrade Lenin, that we will with honour fulfil this thy behest...
>
> Leaving us, comrade Lenin enjoined us to keep the unity of our party as the apple of our eye. We vow to thee, comrade Lenin, that we will with honour also fulfil this thy behest...
>
> Leaving us, comrade Lenin enjoined us to keep and strengthen the dictatorship of the proletariat. We vow to thee, comrade Lenin, that we will not spare our strength also to fulfil with honour this thy behest...
>
> Leaving us, comrade Lenin enjoined us to strengthen with all our might the union of workers and peasants. We vow to thee, comrade Lenin, that we will with honour also fulfil this thy behest...
>
> Leaving us, comrade Lenin enjoined us to remain loyal to the principles of the Communist International. We vow to thee, comrade Lenin, that we will not spare our lives to strengthen and extend the union of the toilers of the whole world — the Communist International.

Pravda, 30 January 1924

This sort of image was much more appropriate to the prevailing Party mood than were those of Trotsky and Zinoviev. As this type of symbolism became rooted in the Soviet political process, even someone of the stature of Bukharin found it difficult to shake. When the Stalin cult burst onto the scene in December 1929, it was connected to that of Lenin. Symbolically, Stalin had been able to root himself in the cult of Lenin and thus assume unimpeachable authority: he was the 'continuer' and best pupil of Lenin, and thereby inherited his authority.

PROBLEMS AND ISSUES
- Ideology
- Modernisation
- Role of the party

Another source of support for Stalin in the Party was the positions that he espoused. The notion of socialism in one country was important in this way because it constituted a recognition that Russia could build socialism alone without having to rely on outside assistance. This gave a sense of meaning to those who had joined the Party and thereby committed themselves to the achievement of socialism in Russia. Unlike the doctrine of world revolution, which seemed to promise nothing but continued waiting for rescue by the proletariat of the West, this promised success through their own efforts. It thus tapped into nationalist sentiments. Similarly, Stalin's break with the gradualism of the NEP at the end of the decade struck a responsive chord. For many in the party the NEP had become a dead end; there seemed no way of loosening the capitalist grip that the NEP embodied and therefore no means of achieving socialism while relying on the petit bourgeois peasantry. The smashing of this reliance, through increased industrialisation and ultimately agricultural collectivisation, revived for many the sense of commitment and enthusiasm that had been waning. By fostering both of these policies, Stalin would have substantially increased his support in Party ranks.

Another factor generating support for Stalin relates to the appointment process referred to above. The support he was able to consolidate through appointments was reinforced by the way in which successive opposition groups called for greater democracy in the Party and criticised the power and position Party secretaries at all levels enjoyed. Any replacement of appointment by election as the means of filling positions would have called into question their continued power and privileges. As a result, they were encouraged to throw their support behind Stalin, both because he was combatting the opposition groups and because he was the head of the secretarial hierarchy that was under attack.

The Lenin Levy

Stalin's position was also strengthened by changes in Party membership during this period. At the Tenth Congress in 1921, the Party had 732 251 members; by 1930 it had grown to 1 677 910. This net gain of almost one million members, achieved in part through the famous Lenin levies of 1924 and 1925, obscures the fact that the number of people entering the party during this period was actually much higher. Major Party purges had been undertaken in 1921 and 1929–30, resulting in a significant loss of members. The large numbers of people flocking into the Party during this decade were less ideologically aware and often had lower formal educational levels than those who had entered the Party earlier. In addition, the loyalty of these people was under question. They had entered when the Party was a ruling body and when the trials and tribulations of the Civil War had been overcome. Many came from the peasantry, thereby stimulating fears of peasant infection. For these people, the simplified, catechismic Marxism and the mythology of the leader offered by Stalin were very attractive. They could more easily understand and take up the ideology he offered than the message of his opponents. Moreover it was to these people that Stalin's message was directed, unlike his opponents whose main concern was Marxist doctrine itself; many of them thought more about Marxist scholasticism than about getting through to the ill-educated Party masses. Stalin spoke to these new recruits, and many of them responded by supporting him.

The ethos of the Party also assisted Stalin's cause. Most bouts of elite conflict were played out within Party organs, and it was here that Stalin's strength lay. None of the oppositionists made full use of the resources potentially available to them outside the Party: Trotsky and the army, Zinoviev and the Communist International, Tomsky and the trade unions. By remaining within the arena of the Party and allowing themselves always to appear as the opposition to a Stalin-led leadership, successive opposition groups automatically breached the anti-fractional decision of the Tenth Congress. The ethos of Party unity and discipline was incredibly strong, leading Trotsky to declare at the Thirteenth Congress:

> Comrades, none of us wishes to be nor can be right against our party. In the last analysis the party is always right, because the party is the single historical instrument that the proletariat possesses for the fulfilment of its basic tasks... I know that it is impossible to be right against the party. It is possible to be right only with the party and through the party, because history has created no other means for the realisation of what is right. The English have an historical proverb: my country right or wrong. With much greater historical right we can say: right or wrong in particular, specific concrete questions at particular times, but this is my party.

Trinadtsatyi s'ezd RKP(b) Mai 1924 goda: Stenograficheskii otchet, Moscow, 1963, p.158

With Stalin clothed in the garb of Leninist Party leadership and such sentiments prevailing, the opposition could hardly fail to appear in a negative light.

But of course Stalin's great skill in the political arts compared with his opponents must be acknowledged. Initially seen as a mediocrity, and still treated by some as one, Stalin was able to outwit his opponents. He attacked when the time was opportune and he waited when necessary. His timing, his building of alliances and his use of political resources showed a skilled political practitioner at work. In contrast, his opponents appeared clumsy and politically naive. They made many mistakes, failed to take advantage of any opportunities that offered, and fell victims to their own inadequacies.

In sum, Stalin's success was due to more than his control over the appointment apparatus alone. His ability to garner support through a variety of means was the hallmark of his rise to the top. But although Stalin's victory over the right in 1929 seemed to leave him supreme, the events of the 1930s were to show that his position was not yet one of complete security or personal power.

List of references

Deutscher, Isaac, *Stalin*, Penguin, Harmondsworth, 1966, chs. 7 & 8.
Medvedev, Roy, *Let History Judge*, Oxford University Press, Oxford, 1989, ch. 2.

Schapiro, Leonard, *The Communist Party of the Soviet Union*, Methuen, London, 1970, chs. 16 & 20.

Trotsky, Leon, *Stalin. Vol. 2 The Revolutionary in Power*, Panther, London, 1968 (originally published 1947), chs. 12 & 13.

Tucker, Robert, C., *Stalin as Revolutionary 1879–1929*, Chatto & Windus, London, 1974, chs. 9–11.

Essay Questions

1 How well did the structure of the government established by the Bolsheviks and the manner in which it operated in Russia in the decade following the October Revolution conform to Marxist ideology?

2 Why was the question of modernisation so ideologically important for the Communists yet so divisive during the 1920s?

3 Account for the powerful position Stalin had established for himself within the Communist Party by the end of the 1920s.

THE TURBULENT THITIES

THITIES

T HE 1930S saw the Soviet Union wracked by the enormous upheavals of the first five-year-plan and the Great Terror. The socio-economic structure of the country was completely recast, while in the political sphere the dominance of Stalin was firmly established.

Focus questions

In assessing the significance of these upheavals, the following questions may provide a focus:

- How successful was agricultural collectivisation?

- How was cultural life affected by the five-year-plans?
- Why did the Great Terror come about?
- What was the effect of the Great Terror?

THE GREAT TRANSFORMATION

Agricultural Collectivisation

PROBLEMS
AND ISSUES
• Modernisation

Large-scale agricultural collectivisation had begun at the end of 1929 and although this campaign continued in some areas until the late 1930s, by 1933 the battle was well and truly won. The campaign consisted of the destruction of private agriculture through the forcible establishment of collective farms. In practice, this meant the abolition of boundaries between private farms, the consolidation of these separate farms into single large estates, and the reduction of the independent peasantry to the status of tied agricultural workers. But in its implementation, the policy of agricultural collectivisation was much less straightforward than this would suggest.

The decision to embark on total collectivisation had been made without

Following agricultural collectivisation, the main form of agriculture was the collective farm. This picture shows a meeting of the members of a farm in the 1930s (SCR)

the necessary preparatory work being carried out. No regional agricultural surveys were done to provide information that would allow informed decisions about the best means of managing the move to collectivism. There was also a great deal of uncertainty about the form and structure the new collective farms should have. The confusion that resulted was reinforced by the excessive speed with which the government wanted collectivisation to proceed. A CC decision of 5 January 1930 called for collectivisation to be completed in major grain-producing regions like the Lower and Middle Volga and the North Caucasus by autumn 1930 or, at the very latest, spring 1931. In other areas the deadline was autumn 1931 or, at the latest, spring 1932. Demands for increased tempos, the official confusion, the levels of peasant opposition and the wish to avoid being labelled a class enemy or wrecker in the wake of the Shakhty affair, encouraged 'excesses' in the conduct of the campaign.

Rural Opposition

Officially, the campaign was based on the myth of a popular surge of enthusiasm for collectivisation from within the peasant villages. Doubtless in some areas there were poorer peasants who supported the collectivisation campaign. Certainly there was enthusiasm and support among urban workers for this policy; many formed brigades and went into the countryside to help their rural cousins restructure their lives. But within the villages, the overwhelming response was one of, at best, sullen resentment, and at worst, open armed opposition. This sort of peasant reaction was met by armed force. Armed detachments of workers, poor peasants and soldiers were sent to the countryside to force the peasants into the collectives. Villages would be surrounded in the early hours of the morning. Rich peasants and opponents were arrested and taken away, and the remaining peasants moved to the centre of what was to be the new collective farm. Village buildings were often razed, and boundary markers between individual farms were eliminated. Any opposition was brutally suppressed, often with much loss of life.

PROBLEMS AND ISSUES
● Ideology — in theory and practice
● Counter-revolution

Opposition was particularly bitter among the so-called rich peasants, the *kulaks*. The *kulaks* had long been the object of Bolshevik concern. It was believed that they were behind grain strikes in the 1920s which created the shortages in the towns; that they were firmly opposed to Bolshevik rule; and that their prominence in the local community enabled them to turn other peasants against the Bolsheviks. These beliefs encouraged the Bolsheviks to seek to use collectivisation to eradicate this opponent from the Russian countryside; hand in hand with collectivisation went a policy of dekulakisation, or 'the liquidation of the *kulaks* as a class'. The *kulaks* (and this simply became a term to refer to anyone who opposed the Bolsheviks in the countryside whether they were wealthy or poor) had their land, houses and most of their belongings expropriated, and were deported to northern Russia or Siberia. Many died as a direct result of this process; no accurate figures are available, but at least 4.5 million people seem to have been dekulakised.

The disorganisation and chaos that resulted were so great that in March 1930 Stalin called a halt to the speed of collectivisation. In an article entitled 'Dizzy with success', Stalin criticised lower level officials for the pace of collectivisation and for the resultant chaos. The general message that this article conveyed seemed to be that force would no longer be used to conduct collectivisation. The result was that the proportion of the peasantry in the new collective farms* fell by some 60 per cent in three months. The offensive recommenced following the harvest of 1930, however, with coercion again prominent.

'Kill, Kill, Kill'

Peasant opposition remained strong, with numerous cases of armed rebellion having to be suppressed by troops in many parts of the country. More frequently, peasants simply destroyed their produce, livestock and tools rather than surrender them to the state. A particularly graphic description is given by the novelist Mikhail Sholokhov:

> 66 ... livestock began to be slaughtered every night in Gremyachy. Hardly had darkness fallen when the brief and stifled bleating of a sheep, the mortal scream of a pig or the bellowing of a calf would be heard piercing the silence.

---

* Officially there were two types of farms, collective farms and state farms. In both types of farm the land was collectively worked, but in the collective farms the land was formally the property of the farmers whose income was dependent on the farm's output. In the state farms, the state owned the land and paid the farmers a wage.

Not only those who had joined the collective farm, but individual farmers also slaughtered. They killed oxen, sheep, pigs, even cows; they slaughtered animals kept for breeding. In two nights the horned cattle of Gremyachy were reduced to half their number. The dogs began to drag entrails and guts about the village, the cellars and granaries were filled with meat. In two days the co-operative shop sold some two hundred poods* of salt which had been lying in the warehouse for eighteen months. 'Kill, it's not ours now!' 'Kill, they'll take it for the meat collection tax if you don't.' 'Kill, for you won't taste meat in the collective farm.' The insidious rumours crept around. And they killed. They ate until they were unable to move. Everybody, from the youngest to the oldest, suffered with stomach-ache. At dinner-time the tables groaned under the weight of boiled and roasted meat. At dinner-time everybody had a greasy mouth, everybody belched as though they had been at a funeral repast in memory of the dead. And all were owlish with their intoxication of eating.

*A pood was a measure of weight equalling 16.3 kilograms.

Mikhail Sholokhov, *Virgin Soil Upturned*, Penguin, Harmondsworth, 1977, pp.127-8

The economic losses were enormous, as Tables 5.1 and 5.2 show. These tables are based on official Soviet statistics, and it is likely that the drops in production were greater than these figures suggest.

The loss of human life was also extensive. People died not just in opposing collectivisation, but also because excessive state grain procurements left many peasants, even in the collectives, with insufficient food. As the demoralised peasantry worked reluctantly in the new collective farms, they were often unable to produce enough grain both to feed themselves and to meet the state's demands. This was thrown into sharp relief by the famine which struck the Ukraine and the North Caucasus in 1933. Although the harvest in the North Caucasus had been poor, the famine was not a result of natural causes. It was produced by the high levels of grain procurement enforced by the state, which left the peasants with almost nothing to eat. The suffering and death were enormous, and the resistance of the peasantry was broken.

Although collectivisation was pushed through to secure state control over grain production in order to use the surplus to finance industrial development, in the short term the effect of collectivisation was the reverse of that desired. Instead of being the source of funds for industry, agriculture was a net drain on the economy because of the resources that had to be pumped into the countryside to establish and maintain collective agriculture.

PROBLEMS AND ISSUES
- Modernisation
- Role of the party and state

Party Control in the Countryside

In terms of its other main purpose, the establishment of Party control over the peasants and the countryside, collectivisation was successful. Private agriculture was eliminated and although in 1935 peasants were allowed to own private plots of land to grow crops for consumption and sale (by 1937 such plots produced some 50 per cent to 70 per cent of vegetables, fruit, meat and milk), the power of private ownership in the countryside was broken. Land was nationalised, as was much of the livestock, and production targets, delivery

Table 5.1   Level of Agricultural Production

	Index	Percentage change over previous year	Grain harvest (million tonnes)
1913	100		
1928	124	2.5	74.5
1929	121	−2.4	72.8
1930	117	−3.3	84.8
1931	114	−2.6	70.6
1932	107	−6.1	70.7
1933	101	−5.6	69.5
1934	106	5.0	68.7
1935	119	12.3	76.2
1936	109	−8.4	57.0
1937	134	22.9	99.0
1938	120	−10.5	70.1
1939	121	0.8	70.1
1940	141	16.5	97.1

Adapted from Roger A. Clarke & Dubravko J.I. Matko, *Soviet Economic Facts 1917–81*, Macmillan, London, 1983, pp.13 & 146

Table 5.2   Livestock Numbers (in millions)

	Cattle	Pigs	Sheep	Goats
1928	60.1	22.0	97.3	9.7
1929	58.2	19.4	97.4	9.7
1930	50.6	14.2	85.5	7.8
1931	42.5	11.7	62.5	5.6
1932	38.3	10.9	43.8	3.8
1933	33.5	9.9	34.0	3.3
1934	33.5	11.5	32.9	3.6
1935	38.9	17.1	36.4	4.4
1936	46.0	25.9	43.8	6.1
1937	47.5	20.0	24.3	7.2
1938	50.9	25.7	57.3	9.3
1939	53.5	25.2	69.9	11.0
1940	47.8	22.5	66.6	10.1

Clarke & Matko, pp.168, 171 & 174

quotas and prices were all set by the state. Never again could peasant agriculture hold the state to ransom. Furthermore, by herding the peasants into collective farms, the state now had an organisational structure (legally formalised by the Collective Farm Statute of 1935) that enabled the exercise of continuing control over the peasantry. This control was reflected in the introduction of the internal passport in 1932. This document was necessary for all citizens who wished to travel in the USSR, but when it was introduced it was not given to peasants. The peasants were denied the automatic right to leave the collective.

Although collectivisation created the framework for improved Party control in the countryside, it would be a mistake to see this as reflecting an extensive Party presence in the rural areas. The establishment of collective and state farms and of the machine tractor stations to serve them (places where farm machinery was concentrated in order to serve a number of farms) created organisational centres on which the Party could rest in an effort to penetrate rural society. However, Party penetration of the countryside was slow. The number of Party cells in rural areas grew from 30 000 with 404 000 members in mid-1930 to 80 000 with 790 000 members in October 1933. By mid-1932, only 20 per cent of collective farms had a Party cell or organised group of communists. In the Belyi district of Smolensk, there was approximately one Party member for every two collective farms in 1935, while by mid-1936 only four of the 21 Party cells in the district were in rural areas where about 93 per cent of the population lived. The Party remained thinly spread in the countryside.

Review and discuss

- Why did Stalin undertake rapid and forced collectivisation?
- Why was there so much peasant resistance?
- Put yourself in the position of a Russian peasant in the mid 1930s and write a paragraph explaining your attitude to collectivisation.
- Consider other ways in which collectivisation could have been established.

INDUSTRIALISATION

PROBLEMS AND ISSUES

- Modernisation

The upward amendment of plan targets in the rural sector, reflected in the rising tempo of collectivisation, had its counterpart in industry with the slogan 'to complete the five-year-plan in four years'. Unrealistic targets for construction and production were set as pressure was increased to develop industry, and particularly heavy industry, at breakneck speed. The sense of urgency is reflected in a speech by Stalin in February 1931:

> It is sometimes asked whether it is not possible to slow down the tempo somewhat, to put a check on the movement. No, comrades, it is not possible! The tempo must not be reduced! On the contrary, we must increase it as much as is within our powers and possibilities. This is dictated to us by our obligations to the workers and peasants of the USSR. This is dictated to us by our obligations to the working class of the whole world.
>
> To slacken the tempo would mean falling behind. And those who fall behind get beaten. No, we refuse to be beaten! One feature of the history

The pressures for rapid industrialisation are reflected in this anonymous 1930 poster. The poster declares: 'Through an accelerated tempo we will complete the five-year-plan in four years' (Sovietsky Khudoznik Publishers, Moscow)

of old Russia was the continual beatings she suffered because of her backwardness. She was beaten by the Mongol khans. She was beaten by the Turkish beys. She was beaten by the Swedish feudal lords. She was beaten by the Polish and Lithuanian gentry. She was beaten by the British and French capitalists. She was beaten by the Japanese barons. All beat her — because of her backwardness, because of her military backwardness, cultural backwardness, political backwardness, industrial backwardness, agricultural backwardness. They beat her because to do so was profitable and could be done with impunity. You remember the words of the pre-revolutionary poet: 'You are poor and abundant, mighty and impotent, Mother Russia.' Those gentlemen were quite familiar with the verses of the old poet. They beat her, saying: 'You are poor and impotent', so you can be beaten and plundered with impunity. Such is the law of the exploiters — to beat the backward and the weak. It is the jungle law of capitalism. You are backward, you are weak — therefore you are wrong; hence you can be beaten and enslaved. You are mighty — therefore you are right; hence we must be wary of you.

That is why we must no longer lag behind.

Stalin, 'The Tasks of Business Executives', *Works*, Vol.13, pp.40–41

"

Through the widespread mobilisation of labour, the use of 'shock work' tactics and by tapping the reserves of commitment and enthusiasm among leading

In 1929, construction
of the town of
Magnitogorsk and its
steelworks were
begun. Young
workers were
recruited from all
parts of the country.
This group is
travelling by train to
Magnitogorsk in
1930 (Museum of
Modern Art, Oxford)

Magnitogorsk had to
be built from the
ground up. Workers
were initially housed
in tents (Museum of
Modern Art, Oxford)

sections of the working class, mighty advances were achieved in the industrial
sphere. The basic infrastructure for heavy industry was expanded and new
industrial centres, like that at Magnitogorsk in the Urals, rose in formerly
virgin territory. Vast projects like the Dnepr Dam were built, supplying more
power for the fulfilment of the five-year-plan. Engineering and heavy industry
were developed to new heights. Inevitably such development was patchy, both
in terms of its quality and its geographical distribution, and although in many
areas of the economy the exaggerated targets were not met, an enormous leap
forward in the industrial sector was achieved. Its dimensions are suggested
by Table 5.3.

Table 5.3   Industrial Development in the USSR (Soviet Figures)

	Total		Producer goods		Consumer goods	
	Index	Percentage increase over prev. year	Index	Percentage increase over prev. year	Index	Percentage increase over prev. year
1913	100		100		100	
1928	132	18.9	155	21.1	120	17.6
1929	158	19.7	200	29.0	137	14.2
1930	193	22.2	276	38.0	151	10.2
1931	233	20.7	355	28.6	171	13.2
1932	267	14.6	424	19.4	187	9.4
1933	281	5.2	450	6.1	196	4.8
1934	335	19.2	563	25.1	220	12.2
1935	411	22.7	713	26.6	258	17.3
1936	529	28.7	934	31.0	324	25.6
1937	588	11.2	1013	8.5	373	15.1
1938	657	11.7	1138	12.3	415	11.3
1939	763	16.1	1353	18.9	464	11.8
1940	852	11.7	1554	14.9	497	7.1

Clarke & Matko, p.10

Review

- Using information from Table 5.3, sketch graphs that illustrate the growth of the Soviet economy under Stalin.
- Compare the production figures in Tables 5.1 and 5.3. What is the relationship between them? Does this tell us anything about the economic strategy that was adopted?

PROBLEMS AND ISSUES

- Modernisation

Just as in the countryside, these industrial developments had important social implications. The construction of new industrial centres created an enormous demand for labour, which was largely satisfied by displaced peasants; nine million peasants entered the industrial labour force during the first five-year-plan (1928–32). The urban population increased 2.5 times between 1928 and 1940, seriously straining the capacity of the cities and the new industrial enterprises to provide adequate facilities. The Soviet housing shortage stems from this period. Despite the best efforts of authorities, the adequacy of public transport lagged badly behind the demand. Urban health, welfare and education authorities were stretched to the limit. Juvenile delinquency, petty crime, alcoholism and broken marriages abounded. In the factories, the absence of unemployment removed one of the weapons with which the authorities sought to maintain order. As a result, labour discipline was often weak and, despite the efforts of the Stakhanovite movement in 1935–36 to stimulate the workers to greater efforts by providing positive role models, labour productivity remained low.

The development of the coal reserves of the Donets Basin was a major element of the first five-year plan. This 1930 poster by A. Deineka declares: 'Let us mechanise the Donbas' (Sovietsky Khudoznik Publishers, Moscow)

The centrepiece of the first five-year plan was heavy industry. The Stalin metallurgical combine in Kuznetsk was built during this period (SCR)

THE SECOND FIVE-YEAR-PLAN

The economic foundations laid earlier in the decade were extended in the latter part of the 1930s. The second five-year-plan (1933–37) had more realistic targets and emphasised the production of consumer goods. As a result, it was both a consolidation and an extension of the gains made during the first five-year-plan period. By the end of the second plan period, Soviet industry had a record of impressive achievement with significant gains in many areas of production. But there were also shortfalls in many areas, particularly because of the priority given to heavy industry. The production of consumer goods was considered a lower level priority than producer goods, leading to continuing consumer goods shortages in the towns and countryside. Housing remained in short supply, and industrial workers continued to work under significant pressure. Differential wage rates, the Stakhanovite campaign with its ever greater pace of work, and increasingly heavy discipline (e.g. laws that effectively tied workers to their existing jobs) kept the workforce subordinate. But this alone was insufficient to maintain growth rates. In 1937 the growth rate fell, partly due to the Great Terror (see p.125), but also because more resources were directed into the armaments industry as Hitler's Germany seemed increasingly threatening.

In the rural areas, some of the pressure on the peasantry was reduced, at least until 1938. There was no retreat from the collectives and the state continued to take most of the produce at very low prices, but the peasants were allowed some room for economic manoeuvre. They could have private plots and some animals to supplement their incomes by selling their produce in the market. Agriculture slowly recovered as the peasants regained their confidence and the new collectives settled down to a more orderly existence. But agricultural production still failed to meet the targets established in the second five-year-plan. In 1938 the Party began to exert increased pressure on the villages once again. State procurement at low prices was applied to a large range of peasant produce, taxes were increased and the amount of compulsory work on the collective was increased. Such measures were clearly unpopular, and the peasant response can be seen in the production figures for 1938 in Table 5.1.

PROBLEMS AND ISSUES

● Role of the party and state

Despite the difficulties and undoubted social costs, the Soviet economy had clearly experienced dramatic change during the 1930s. By the end of the decade, industry was the dominant sector of the economy and its level of development was much higher than it had been ten years earlier. Agriculture had been reorganised on a collective basis, and although it was still subject to serious technical difficulties that could contribute to crop failure (such as deficient supply systems to the farms), as a structure it was more responsive to the will of the Soviet leaders than it had been previously. Overall, the decade was one of substantial economic advance, although at significant cost.

THE CULTURE OF THE GREAT TRANSFORMATION

**PROBLEMS
AND ISSUES**

● Stalinism

The intense mobilisation for the building of socialism had important consequences for Soviet life, making it increasingly rigid and hierarchical. Inequality and privilege became entrenched. Egalitarianism in wages was rejected in favour of steep wage differentials in accordance with skill and responsibility. Wages were supplemented for those at the top by access to special perks and privileges. Public morality became strict and unbending, as the liberal era of the 1920s was superseded. The family was strengthened as an institution and traditional family values were encouraged; divorce was made difficult to obtain, free marriage was denied its former legal status, and abortion and homosexuality were banned. Discipline, commitment and vigilance became the watchwords, even in matters of culture. Literature, art, the theatre and music were considered valuable and legitimate only if they followed and presented the party line. The notion of 'art for art's sake' had no place in an environment in which writers were to be 'engineers of the human soul' and were to contribute to the construction of the 'new socialist man'. Creativity and innovation were replaced by conformity in the cultural sphere.

There was also a significant change in approach to history at this time. The populist focus of earlier historiography was now overshadowed by an emphasis upon the development and growth of the Russian state. The expansion and strengthening of the Russian state was seen as a positive force in history rather than the backward and obscurantist structure it had been deplored as in the 1920s. In accord with this, a new positive emphasis was given to the great state-makers of Russian history. People like Ivan the Terrible and Peter the Great were celebrated in both scholarly and popular spheres; perhaps the best instance of this changed focus was Eisenstein's famous film *Alexander Nevsky* produced in 1938.

The historically positive role that the Russian state was now believed to have played in history was reflected in the changed attitude to the historical relationship between the Russian and non-Russian peoples of the USSR. Russian colonialism and domination were declared to have been progressive in drawing these backward people into a more advanced level of development that culminated in the socialist revolution. This ideology laid the basis for the theme of the unity of the peoples of the USSR, foreshadowing the notion of Soviet patriotism that was to become so important during World War II.

The emphasis on the commitment to building socialism and on the Russian state-makers of the past was echoed in the emergence in the press of popular folk heroes. These were individuals from all walks of life who were held up as examples for the rest of the population to emulate. The most important of these was Alexei Stakhanov, a miner who exceeded his work norm (how much coal he was expected to mine) fourteen-fold and was thenceforth held up as a model worker. He was the focus of the Stakhanovite campaign noted on p.115. But public attention and interest was probably caught far more by the exploits of Soviet aviators and Arctic explorers, which received wide publicity in the press. A young boy, Pavlik Morozov, who denounced his father for being involved in a kulak plot and was killed by angry relatives, became a model for all to follow because he had put the building of socialism above family concerns. All of these model citizens were publicly linked to Stalin; they attributed their performance to his care and guidance. The emergence of these folk heroes was thus an important means of confirming the 'great man' emphasis of contemporary history and the Stalin cult. It also helped to legitimise the notions of inequality and of personal commitment to the building of socialism.

Thus as the economy and social structure underwent revolutionary change, the public environment became much more conservative. Hierarchy, discipline, authority and the state were projected into a central place in Soviet life.

Discuss

- Consider the relationship between pressures for economic development and a more conservative public sphere of life.

THE EMERGENCE OF THE NEW ELITE

PROBLEMS AND ISSUES
- Modernisation
- Revolution

The massive economic changes set in train at the end of the 1920s were accompanied by large-scale social mobility. The transformation of peasants into factory workers was the first step for millions in the climb up the social ladder. The move into the factory was followed for many by promotion into lower level administrative and managerial positions which, if the individuals were sufficiently talented and fortunate, could lead to the attainment of high office. One of the principal avenues of such mobility was education. Doubts about the reliability of the bourgeois specialists, reflected most graphically in the Shakhty affair of 1928 and the trials of engineers and specialists in 1930 (particularly the trial of the so-called Industrial Party), led to pressures within the system for the training of Soviet technical cadres. Educational facilities, especially technical education, were accordingly expanded and the doors of educational institutions thrown open to young workers and party members. On completion of their education, many of these people moved into administrative and managerial positions created by the expanding economic structure.

PROBLEMS AND ISSUES
- Modernisation
- Role of the party

Another important avenue of upward mobility was the Party. Over the decade, Party membership increased substantially, as Table 5.4 shows:

The Industrial Party Trial was held in Moscow in November and December 1930. The defendants were accused of industrial sabotage, wrecking and espionage. Here they hear the death penalty, which was later commuted (Archiv Gerstenberg)

T.H. Rigby, *Communist Party Membership in the USSR 1917–1967*, Princeton University Press, Princeton, 1968, p.52

Table 5.4   Communist Party Membership

1929	1 535 362	1935	2 358 714
1930	1 677 910	1936	2 076 842
1931	2 212 225	1937	1 981 697
1932	3 117 250	1938	1 920 002
1933	3 555 338	1939	2 306 973
1934	2 701 008	1940	3 399 975

The overall expansion was significant, particularly considering the extent of membership loss associated with the purge of 1933–34, the membership screenings of 1935 and 1936, and the 1936–38 Terror. Recruits flowed into the Party in the early part of the decade when there was a clear need for more Party functionaries to exercise control over the expanding economic apparatus; the Party wanted members in all of the new factories and farms to ensure Party control. Those who showed initiative and political sense rose rapidly through the ranks, especially if they had some technical education qualifications. Future leading figures like Khrushchev, Brezhnev, Kosygin and Gromyko all made massive strides in their careers in the 1930s. But it was not only the opportunities made possible through the expansion of the economic and political apparatus associated with the great transformation that made their rise possible. Important too was the effect of the Great Terror (see p.125). By decimating much of the political and economic elite, the Terror created vacancies that this ascendant group could fill, and it thereby boosted their passage up the social and political ladder. The combined effect of the system's expansion plus the Terror facilitated extremely rapid and widespread mobility.

From the outset the Bolsheviks had recognised the importance of education. This poster from 1920 by A. Radakov concerns illiteracy. The main message says: 'Being illiterate is the same as being blind. All around him waits failure and unhappiness' (Sovietsky Khudoznik Publishers, Moscow)

The rise to power of this new elite during the 1930s is very important. It brought into leading positions people whose social origins lay in the villages and in the workers' quarters of the towns. They were representatives of the classes that traditionally had been exploited. This constituted a real social revolution with the dispossessed classes now producing those who dominated the society.

One reflection of this may have been the cultural decline and conformity discussed above. While this has often been attributed to Stalin personally, this emergent elite also had a part to play. Mostly educated in technical fields, with the quality of the education frequently suspect, and coming from a background with little appreciation of literature, art and music, it is not surprising that this group had little time for these aspects of Russian culture. The imposition of conservative norms, the elimination of experimentation and the tying of culture to socialist construction fitted in with the prevailing outlook of this group. Rising out of social and economic hardship, it is probably also not surprising that this group embraced privilege so enthusiastically and firmly embedded it in the system. As they rose up the hierarchy and gained increased access to the good life in terms of housing, food supplies, holidays and consumer goods, they became firm supporters of the system that provided them with such benefits. Not only did this group become consolidated as the arbiters of the Soviet future, but the structure of inequality which served their interests also became solidly entrenched.

POLITICS IN THE PARTY

PROBLEMS AND ISSUES

• Role of the party

Stalin's victory over the Right Opposition in 1929 had made him the predominant figure in the leadership. The Politburo elected in July 1930 after the Fifteenth Congress was filled by those who had supported Stalin in the conflicts of the 1920s. Rykov was the only former oppositionist to retain a seat (and then only until December 1930), and he was there purely for symbolic purposes, to give the impression of unanimity. But Stalin's defeat of the right did not mean that he was unchallenged. Three groups emerged in the early years of the decade criticising the policies associated with Stalin and calling for his removal. These were the Syrtsov-Lominadze group in 1930 and in 1932 the Riutin Platform and the Eismont-Tolmachev-Smirnov group. The most important of these was the Riutin Platform. This was a stinging indictment of Stalin and his policies, and demanded his removal. At a meeting of the Politburo, Stalin demanded Riutin's death, but the Politburo refused. Riutin was arrested and sent into confinement. The Riutin affair demonstrates two things: the existence within leading Party circles of considerable uneasiness with Stalin, and that Stalin was not able to get his way on all issues. There were still limits to Stalin's power and authority.

Stalin (second from right) with close supporters of the early 1930s — Kalinin, Kaganovich, Orzhonikidze and Voroshilov (Life Picture Service)

This uneasiness in the upper levels of the Party is significant in the context of continuing uneasiness at lower levels of the Party as well. Party leaders at regional levels and lower had to bear the brunt of the campaign for agricultural collectivisation. They were caught between the demands of the centre for higher levels of performance and successful completion of collectivisation on the one hand, and the opposition of the peasants on the other. They knew from

first-hand experience what a close run thing collectivisation had been. They were also the ones who were forced to carry the blame for the mistakes and excesses of collectivisation, despite the fact that many of them had urged moderation. The experience of being made scapegoats was firmly established in their minds.

The 1933–34 Party Purge

These feelings were strengthened by the Party purge of 1933–34. The purge was designed generally to cleanse the Party of 'all unreliable, unstable and hanger-on elements'. More specifically it was directed against double-dealers who deceived the Party and sought to undermine its policy, and those who discredited state and Party decisions by questioning their practicability: the 'enemies with a Party card in their pockets' (CC decisions entitled 'O chistke partii', *Pravda*, 13 January and 29 April 1933). These categories seemed to apply directly to those lower level Party leaders who had urged moderation during collectivisation and whose performance in that campaign was deemed to be deficient. Most such leaders were able to deflect the purge away from their own positions, but they saw the purge as an attempt by the centre to establish tighter control over them. The resentment thus created fed into the proceedings of the Seventeenth Congress of the Party in January–February 1934.

Labelled the 'Congress of Victors', the Seventeenth Congress was held at a time when the general line of the Party seemed to have been proved correct. The previous harvest had been adequate and industrial development was proceeding apace. Over the previous six months there had been a general relaxation in domestic policy and in the atmosphere in society. There was disquiet with Stalin, however, at the Congress. This was not reflected in open speeches, but there was considerable whispering and complaining among delegates in the corridors about the need to replace Stalin with someone more moderate in outlook. The person usually identified as the desirable replacement was Leningrad Party boss Sergei Kirov, although an examination of his past does not show him to be any more moderate in outlook than most of his colleagues in the leadership. The Congress did register one sign of discontent with Stalin: in the election for membership of the CC, some 270 delegates voted against Stalin. Although this was not nearly enough to prevent his election, in a context where unanimous votes were the norm, it does reflect serious misgivings about Stalin among Party members.

THE KIROV ASSASSINATION

The event that, for many students of Soviet history, is crucial in the unfolding of the 1930s was the assassination of Kirov on 1 December 1934. Many of the details of this event remain obscure, but it is certain that his assassination occurred under very odd circumstances. The assassin, Leonid Nikolaev, was

The assassination of Leningrad boss Sergei Kirov in December 1934 was an important turning point in Soviet political development. His coffin was carried by (among others): from left Vyacheslav Molotov, Kliment Voroshilov, Joseph Stalin and Mikhail Kalinin (New York Public Library)

arrested with a gun and a map of Kirov's route to work in his possession, but he was released and apparently not placed under surveillance. At the time of Kirov's assassination, his bodyguards were all absent. The officer personally responsible for Kirov's safety was killed in an accident before he could give any evidence. Those responsible for Kirov's security (and therefore clearly deficient in the pursuit of their duties) were given only light punishments for their failures. These facts suggest higher level involvement in the assassination. But who was thus involved?

Many have argued that the responsibility lay with Stalin, that he used the Kirov assassination to get rid of a rival and to create a basis on which he could unleash the Terror. If Stalin planned the Terror this far in advance; if he saw Kirov as a rival; and if the security apparatus (the NKVD, successor to the OGPU) could not act independently of Stalin, this interpretation is plausible. However an investigation undertaken at the end of the 1980s provided no conclusive proof of Stalin's responsibility.

Another suggestion is that this action was undertaken by the NKVD itself in an attempt to reverse the decline in their fortunes that was associated with the general relaxation in society and the reorganisation (and formal limitation) to which they had been subject in 1934. An attack on Kirov's life may have been seen by elements in the security apparatus as the excuse they needed to confirm their importance to the regime. Such an interpretation of independent NKVD action would be even more plausible if Trotsky was correct in suggesting that what was intended was an unsuccessful attempt on Kirov's life, not his assassination. Unfortunately, there is insufficient evidence to be sure about either of these interpretations.

What is clear is that the Kirov assassination gave a fillip to the search for enemies in the Party that had been an element of the 1933–34 purge. In

PROBLEMS
AND ISSUES
- Ideology — in
  theory and
  practice
- Counter-revolution

the immediate aftermath of Kirov's death, Stalin introduced an 'extraordinary law' that denied those accused of terrorist activity any protection in the investigation of the charges, while the investigation was to be conducted as soon as possible and followed by immediate execution. For the first time in Soviet history, Party membership was no longer a defence against the death penalty for wrongdoing. This law was followed by the trial of Zinoviev, Kamenev and some of their supporters, all of whom were found guilty of maintaining a secret centre of opposition in Moscow; of deceiving the Party through false repentance for past crimes; and of 'ideological' influence on Kirov's assassin. All were imprisoned. In May 1935 a campaign for the verification of Party documents was launched, followed in 1936 by a campaign for the exchange of Party documents. Both campaigns were designed to improve the chaotic record-keeping system in the Party and to tighten the links between the centre and the regions. But both were also linked to the search for hidden enemies inside the Party.

THE GREAT TERROR

It was within this context of the search for hidden enemies inside the Soviet regime — a concern that went back explicitly to the Shakhty affair but that also had its echoes in earlier worries about petit bourgeois infection and degeneration — that the Terror was unleashed. The class enemy remained undefeated, as the following extract from a Party document of July 1936 demonstrates:

PROBLEMS
AND ISSUES
- Ideology
- Counter-revolution

66 These facts show that the trotskyite-zinovievite counter-revolutionary centre and its leaders, Trotsky, Zinoviev and Kamenev, finally slid down into the swamp of White Guardism, joined forces with the most desperate and embittered enemies of the Soviet power, and turned into the organising force of the remnants of the classes which had been smashed in the USSR and which in desperation are resorting to the terror — the basest instrument of struggle against the Soviet government.

Not only have they turned into the organising force of the remnants of the classes which have been smashed in the USSR, but they have also become the leading detachment of the counter-revolutionary bourgeoisie outside the boundaries of the Union, voicing its will and its aspirations.

All of their activities serve to inspire the worst elements of the white emigration, which is in the service of the foreign secret police and is organised into terrorist groupings abroad, such as ROVS (The Russian Military Union), the Russian Fascist Party, the Fascist Union of Youth, etc.

They have turned into the organising force of the worst and most embittered enemies of the USSR because they have no political motivations for struggling against the party and the Soviet power other than naked and undisguised careerism and the desire to sneak into power at whatever cost.

Confronted with the indisputable triumphs of socialist construction, they first hoped that our party would be unable to cope with its difficulties, as a result of which would be created the possible conditions for their emergence into the open and their attainment of power. But, seeing that the party is successfully overcoming its difficulties, they are wagering on the defeat of the Soviet power in the forthcoming war, as a result of which they dream of attaining power.

And, finally, seeing no prospects at all, in desperation they seize upon the ultimate instrument of struggle — terror.

Whereas previously the trotskyite-zinovievite groups justified their struggle against the party by maintaining, as it were, that the party and government were carrying out an incorrect policy, were leading the country to destruction, now they put forward quite contrary motivations. Now they consider the principal motive for adopting terror to be precisely the successes of our party on all fronts of socialist construction — successes which arouse resentment in them and incite them to revenge for their own political bankruptcy.

99

Secret CC circular, 'On the Terrorist Activities of the Trotskyite-Zinovievite Counter-Revolutionary Bloc', 29 July 1936, *Resolutions and Decisions of the Communist Party*, Vol.3, *The Stalin Years: 1929–1953*, University of Toronto Press, Toronto, 1974, pp.176–7

The Terror lasted from 1936 through 1938 and reached its fiercest intensity during the so-called 'Ezhovshchina' (named after the head of the NKVD, Nikolai Ezhov) of 1937. The public highlights were three show trials of Old Bolsheviks: of Zinoviev, Kamenev and others in August 1936; of Pyatakov, Radek and others in January 1937; and of Bukharin, Rykov, Yagoda and others in March 1938. During these trials the defendants confessed to a whole range of implausible charges, including sabotage, wrecking, spying for foreign powers, seeking

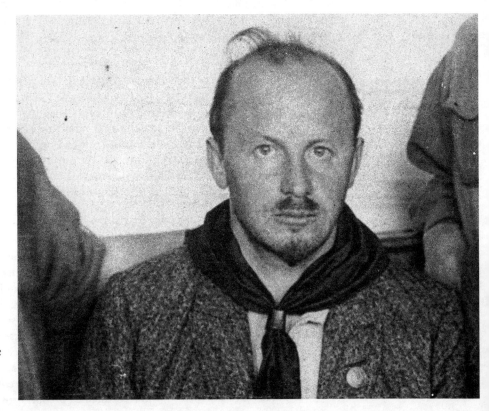

Bukharin was one of the Old Bolsheviks persecuted in the late 1930s. He was executed in 1938 (UPI/Bettmann)

to overthrow the Soviet government, and even to carve up the USSR and sell sections to foreign powers. All defendants were found guilty and executed.

PROBLEMS
AND ISSUES

- Stalinism as
  totalitarianism

But the trials were only the most public face of the terror. The Terror affected millions of Soviet citizens, both prominent and unknown in the West. At the height of the Ezhovshchina, an orgy of denunciations and arrests led to the decimation of the major structures of Soviet society. At all levels of society, in all walks of life, people were arrested and either executed or placed in prison or labour camp. In the camps, people were used as forced labour to work on major construction projects, in the mines, and at other difficult and heavy work. Much of the purging seems to have been arbitrary, with no one apparently safe. While those closest to Stalin among the full members of the Politburo survived, the elite organs were decimated. According to Khrushchev, 70 per cent of the CC elected in 1934 were arrested and shot, while 56 per cent of the delegates to the Seventeenth Congress were arrested. In addition, some 80 per cent of government ministers were purged while in the army three of the five marshals, three of four first rank commanders, all 12 second rank commanders and 60 of the 67 corps commanders were purged. Virtually all Party and state leaders in the Soviet republics were purged, as were many managers and technical specialists in the economy and many who had (even legitimate) contacts abroad. Even the NKVD, which conducted the terror, was itself purged following the replacement of Ezhov by Beria in December 1938.

The exact number who suffered during the Terror is unknown, with estimates ranging from hundreds of thousands to about 15 million. This is discussed in Case Study 5. According to the leading student of the Terror, Robert Conquest, between 1936 and 1938, seven to nine million people were arrested and one to two million shot. Conquest argues that by 1938 between eight and 12 million people were in the camps, of whom a million died each year because of the conditions they had to endure. Everyone in the Soviet Union knew someone who was caught up in the Terror.

The course of the Terror did not proceed without opposition. There is no evidence of any attempt through the use of force either to topple Stalin or to halt the Terror, but there was opposition voiced to the continuation of the Terror at the February–March 1937 CC plenum. This opposition, led by Pavel Postyshev, involved a number of members of the CC and was sufficiently strong to have prevented the body as a whole from coming out in open, unambiguous support of the Terror. There may also have been some opposition at the January 1938 CC plenum, but the evidence is more uncertain for this.

Review

- Read Arthur Koestler's *Darkness at Noon*. What insights does it give you into the Terror?
- Put yourself in the position of a young Russian worker and Communist Party member in the 1930s. Write a paragraph explaining your attitude to Stalin's purges.

Why did the Great Terror Occur?

There is no universally accepted explanation for the Terror. Some have sought to blame Stalin alone, given his mistrust and suspicions about opposition to him inside the Party. Having failed to eliminate his opponents through other means, it is charged, he turned to the gun. Clearly, Stalin must bear a significant part of the responsibility. His enemies, both from the 1920s and the 1930s, were major targets of the Terror; the first show trial was used once and for all to exorcise Trotskyism from the USSR by discrediting Trotsky through the defendants. Stalin was personally involved to the extent of signing numerous lists of names of people to be arrested. Moreover given Stalin's position in the political system in the first half of the 1930s, it is inconceivable that the Terror could have occurred had he opposed it. Nevertheless a focus on Stalin alone is inadequate. It explains neither the extent of the Terror nor why so many people were willing to go along with it. Broader social and institutional factors were important here.

At least five factors were relevant:

Opportunities for social mobility: At worst, denunciation of people and involvement in the Terror and, at best, keeping one's head down and avoiding involvement were encouraged by the hope of personal gain at the expense of others. Every person arrested or killed had to be replaced; when the boss disappeared, someone was promoted to take his place. There were many instances of people denouncing others and then taking over their jobs. This process implicated many people in the Terror.

Target fulfilment mentality: Individual police and informers had quotas of victims to fulfil, just as workers in factories and peasants on farms had their own production quotas. Achieving, and perhaps more importantly

Stalin and four close supporters in 1938. Left to right: Bulganin, Zhdanov, Stalin, Voroshilov and Khrushchev (Staatsbibliothek)

overfulfilling, one's quota was the best hope of avoiding the charge of being a hidden enemy (although even this was often not sufficient). Such an ethos clearly encouraged the continuing expansion of the Terror.

Institutional competition: The Terror may have been seen by the NKVD as an opportunity to establish their primacy over the Party and state and become the leading institution in the system.

Inertia: Denunciation and investigation led to the incrimination of other people. Those incriminated had to be investigated, otherwise the officials laid themselves open to charges of sabotage and wrecking. During interrogation, others were incriminated. The process built upon itself.

Fear: Many people tried to avoid trouble by not becoming involved. Fear paralysed many and insensitised them to what was happening.

Whatever weight one attributes to these different explanations, the result of the Terror is clear: Stalin was established as the unchallenged power in the land.

Discuss

- Discuss the argument that the Terror was the political counterpart of the economic transformation at the beginning of the decade.

THE CULT OF STALIN

PROBLEMS AND ISSUES
- Stalinism as totalitarianism

Stalin's authority had also been built up during this decade through the growing cult of the leader. The Stalin cult had burst onto the public scene in December 1929. During the 1930s the cult continued to expand, both in terms of its saturation of the media and of the claims it made for Stalin. As the cult grew, the figure of Lenin, which had been prominent in its early stages, receded as Stalin became the most important symbol of the regime. He was projected as the source of all inspiration and initiative in Soviet society, the sole source of authority and orthodoxy. Everything had to be justified by reference to Stalin's words. There was even a quasi-religious element in the cultist image. *Pravda* reported the sentiments of two collective farmers in 1935: 'My heart thumped joyfully when I saw that comrade Stalin was coming toward me' (*Pravda*, 7 July 1935); while on leaving Stalin another reported: 'On the stairs I began to run, just like a youth; and joy and pride were in me, that he saw how I managed, and he was pleased' (*Pravda*, 17 May 1935).

A message from the inhabitants of Dagestan declared:

    " Your speech, like a guiding star, lights up our path. If the songs of our bards can delight your hearing — take them. If the sculptures and pictures of our artists can make your eyes happy — accept them. If our lives are demanded by you for the defence of the motherland — take them. One thought inspires us: that if only a small line reached your ears. Whenever we think that you — Stalin — read these lines, strength fills our muscles, heads are raised, and eyes burn strongly. **,,**

Pravda, 24 June 1935

Stalin's image dominated Soviet society, leaping from the pages of newspapers and other publications and staring down at people from billboards, statues and paintings. Stalin became, symbolically, the ultimate source of authority.

FOREIGN POLICY

During the 1920s, foreign policy had been partly shaped by domestic elite conflict. Stalin was locked into a disastrous China policy in the 1920s because Trotsky's criticism of that policy meant that any change would have seemed to be a recognition that Trotsky was right and Stalin wrong. Similarly, the Soviet attacks on social democrats in the West in 1929 and 1930, and the policy of forbidding local Communist Parties in Europe and elsewhere from entering alliances with social democratic and labour parties were linked with the struggle against Bukharin and rightist moderation in the USSR. This line remained unchanged after Hitler and the Nazis came to power in Germany in 1933. Indeed, it may even have assisted Hitler's rise by preventing German Communists from co-operating with the social democrats to oppose him.

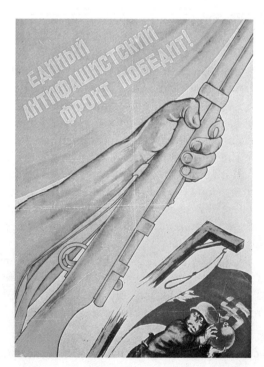

In the mid-1930s, a major aim of Soviet foreign policy was to construct an anti-German alliance. This poster from 1938 by B. Prorokov declares: 'The united anti-fascist front will be victorious! Workers, peasants and labourers of all countries! Widen and strengthen the national front of struggle against fascism and war' (Sovietsky Khudoznik Publishers, Moscow)

There was no change in this line until the Seventh Congress of the Communist International (the international organisation of Communist Parties that was run from Moscow) in July 1935. The Congress launched the Anti-Fascist Popular Front tactic, an attempt to establish anti-fascist alliances between local Communist Parties and other parties to their right. There was a good deal of popular sympathy for this policy in the West where concern about the Nazis was well established. The counterpart to this policy was a Soviet search for a collective treaty with Western states to contain the Nazi menace. Such a policy seemed increasingly attractive to many in the West, particularly given the introduction of the new 'Stalin Constitution' in 1936 which gave the USSR the formal appearance of democracy, and the Soviet assistance to the Spanish Republicans in the Spanish Civil War. But no collective security arrangement was reached, principally because of British and French reluctance to ally themselves with the Soviet Union.

The Nazi-Soviet Pact

The reluctance of the Western powers to come to an arrangement with the USSR prompted Stalin to enter secret negotiations with Hitler in an effort to guarantee Soviet security. The result was the Nazi–Soviet Pact (often called the Molotov–Ribbentrop Pact after the respective foreign ministers) of August 1939. This pact opened the door for Soviet territorial expansion through the incorporation of eastern Poland, the Baltic states (Estonia, Latvia and Lithuania), Rumanian Bessarabia and parts of Finland into the USSR. The incorporation of these areas was followed by their 'pacification', principally through the deportation of all of those who opposed Soviet rule.

Foreign Minister Molotov signing the Frontier and Friendship Treaty between the USSR and Germany, 23 August 1939. This paved the way for the German attack on Poland and the consequent outbreak of World War II (Popperfoto)

Soviet territorial acquisitions prior to the outbreak of the Great Patriotic War (World War II)

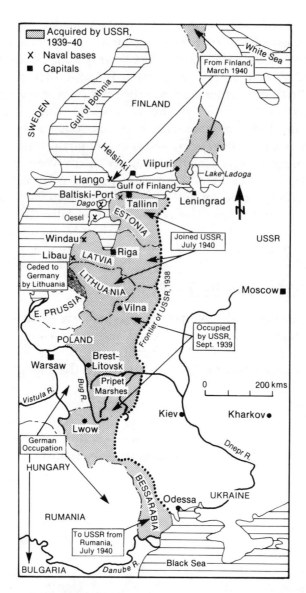

The Nazi–Soviet Pact has been widely condemned in the West as precipitating the outbreak of World War II. Such a criticism is shortsighted. The pact was the culmination of Stalin's search for some form of collective security arrangement to guarantee Soviet borders. The West had been reluctant to enter into any such arrangement. Indeed, their basic hostility to the USSR is reflected in the fact that plans were made to send forces to help the Finns against the Soviet forces on the eve of the German attack on France. The fact that Stalin did not make the best use of the time he gained through the pact does not mean that the pact was not entered into as a defensive precaution.

The Soviet Union also sought to gain extra territory from Finland. Stalin wanted to move the border back further from Leningrad to make it less vulnerable, and to have a base at the mouth of the Gulf of Finland. Finnish refusal led to the outbreak of conflict in 1939. In this short war the inadequacies of the Soviet military, still stunned by the effect of the Terror on its leading ranks, was shown. Although ultimately the Finns were forced to sue for peace, the Soviet victory was very hard won. It showed both Hitler and the West that the Soviet military was not as formidable as some had believed.

Discuss

● Discuss the proposition that once the Communist Party came to power it was inevitable that terror would be employed as a routine administrative means of controlling the peoples of the Soviet Union. This was because central to the ideology of the Communist Party — Marxism — was the concept of class struggle accompanied by the need to employ terror against the class enemy.

CASE STUDY 5

The Debate over the Great Terror

PROBLEMS AND ISSUES

● Stalinism as totalitarianism

The Great Terror has always been seen as one of the most important episodes in Soviet history. It was the sort of development which was seen as being characteristic of a totalitarian regime and, at the same time, as being almost incomprehensible. Nevertheless, for a long time there has been an established historical 'orthodoxy' concerning the Terror. This orthodoxy became the dominant view in the 1960s, principally through the work of Robert Conquest. In the 1980s, this orthodoxy came under challenge, mainly from a group of younger scholars. This debate is the subject of this case study. The first attack came from the work of J. Arch Getty. The main difference between the two approaches lies not in the uncovering of new facts, but in how developments which both sides agree happened should be interpreted. In other words, there is agreement about the sequence of events, but differences about how they should be interpreted. (Publications mentioned are listed at the end.)

Here is a brief review of the events comprising the Great Terror. All accounts agree upon the existence in 1932 of a shadowy opposition to Stalin in the upper reaches of the party, represented by the Riutin Platform. This was followed by the 1933–34 Party purge (*chistka*). The official targets of the purge were 'all unreliable, unstable, and hanger-on elements'. More specifically, these people were described as class alien and hostile elements who had entered the Party, double-dealers who deceive the Party, violators of Party and state discipline who do not carry out decisions and seek to discredit those decisions by questioning their practicality, degenerates who have merged with bourgeois elements, careerists, and moral degenerates. In the middle of this purge, the Seventeenth Congress of the Party was held at which, despite some uneasiness about Stalin, he was re-elected to leadership of the Party.

In December 1934 Kirov was assassinated. This was followed by the extraordinary measures allowing immediate execution of those accused of terrorism, and by the arrest of thousands of people in the Leningrad region on the pretext of their connection with the assassination. Among those arrested were Zinoviev and Kamenev. In 1935 a new campaign was launched, for the verification of Party documents. This was to involve all Party members presenting their Party membership cards to Party authorities who were to check these with Party records. Those members whose performance was deemed to be inadequate or whose record was irregular were to be expelled from the Party. The campaign was presented as an attempt to regularise Party membership records and procedures, but with a view to eliminating from Party ranks any people who did not belong.

This was followed in 1936 by another campaign, for the exchange of Party documents. Officially this was to be a means of getting rid of 'passive' people from the Party. Again, members were to hand in their Party cards to the authorities who would survey their performance and return the cards to those who merited continued Party membership. Between 1936 and 1938 the Terror unrolled. Three show trials of leading political figures occurred in 1936, 1937 and 1938, but at lower levels the purging process extended far more widely. The Terror began to wind down following the replacement of Nikolai Ezhov, head of the NKVD (security apparatus/secret police), with Lavrenty Beria in late 1938. The Eighteenth Congress in March 1939 formally ended the Terror, noting in passing that some excesses had taken place.

How do the different approaches interpret this sequence of events?

The Established Orthodoxy

The orthodox interpretation of these events has Stalin at its centre. The purge of 1933–34 is seen as an attempt to get rid of opponents in the Party, reflecting the uncertainty created in Stalin's mind by the Riutin Platform. This uncertainty was compounded by the reservations about Stalin evident at the Seventeenth Congress. Stalin's response to the emergence of a potential challenger in the guise of Kirov was to plan and execute the assassination of the Leningrad leader. He then used this event to mount the purges, which advanced in increasing levels of intensity as time passed. There was, therefore, a direct link running through the 1933–34 purge, Kirov assassination, the arrests in 1935, the verification and exchange of Party documents, and the Terror.

What ties these events together is the role of Stalin. He is seen as the prime mover behind each of these developments, motivated by the desire to remove enemies and thereby consolidate his position. Stalin is depicted as petty, mean and suspicious, and unwilling to accept any possibility of challenge to his rule. He is shown as having planned the whole broad process, at least from the Kirov assassination, with the aim of completely subordinating all people and institutions to his will.

This general outline has been shared in its essentials by most established Western scholars. Paradoxically, it also became the main line of interpretation in the Soviet Union, chiefly as a result of Khrushchev's secret speech. It is the interpretation adopted in the standard history of the Communist Party by Leonard Schapiro; the major biographer of Stalin, Robert Tucker; and in the chief analysis to come out of the Soviet Union by Roy Medvedev. All agree on Stalin's primary role and, a little more ambiguously, the basic unity of the process, although there are some differences in the evaluations of Stalin's state of mind and mental health.

The Revisionist Interpretation

The most extended piece of revisionist scholarship is that by Getty, although Gabor Rittersporn has also published an important book in this vein. Getty's account differs from the orthodoxy in three main ways.

1 Getty argues that Stalin's personal and institutional power was much more restricted than the orthodox view suggests, and that he was much more a reactive politician during the 1930s, responding to events and other people, than he was an initiator. This means that Stalin did not carefully plan out the Terror in advance, and Getty argues that there is no firm evidence of Stalin's responsibility for Kirov's death. Certainly he acknowledges that Stalin was responsible for launching and continuing the Terror, but this was not the result of an elaborate prior plan.

2 Getty shows that the ability of the centre to control lower level Party organs was very much more restricted than the orthodox view suggests. He argues that the Terror was in part designed to break the power of regional political machines and bring them more firmly under the centre's control. Thus, instead of reflecting the strength of the central apparatus, the Terror showed its weakness.

3 Getty challenges the essential unity of the process from 1933–39. He argues that the 1933–34 purge, and in particular the verification and exchange, were not political but administrative in nature. They were not designed to seek out enemies in the party, but to overcome administrative short-comings in the operation of the Party apparatus. These were house-cleaning operations, designed to clearly establish who was a Party member and who was not, and to get rid of those who did not deserve to be a member as a result of their performance or personal deficiencies (but not political opposition). This is very different from the political aims of the Terror, and therefore there is no automatic progression from the developments of the first part of the 1930s into the Terror.

Orthodoxy or Revisionism?

How are these different accounts to be evaluated? The emphasis on Stalin in the orthodox interpretation clearly recognises the important role he played in the events of the 1930s, including the Terror. It is unlikely, however, that it could be proved that Stalin planned the Terror well in advance. The Soviet archives have not yet produced any solid evidence of such a plan, nor has investigation proved his responsibility for the Kirov assassination. Certainly, if one assumes that Stalin wanted supreme power and was willing to do anything for it, it would be consistent to assume that he planned the course of developments. However, the Terror can be explained without having to resort to this view of Stalin's foreplanning. Indeed, such a view assumes that Stalin had both more foresight than would be reasonable and was able to guide the course of developments in his own interests. But if he was able to dominate events already, why did he need more power? Stalin certainly took advantage of developments and sought to get rid of opposition, but there was no grand plan for the 1930s that unrolled inevitably at his direction.

The ability of the centre to control the lower level Party organs was more restricted than many of the orthodox writers suggest, as I have argued elsewhere. Stalin's personal machine at the centre could not control what Party leaders in the regions were doing. There was no continuing control over regional Party leaders and organisations. The Party in the 1930s was not a smoothly integrated political machine. Central Party organs conducted a long and exhaustive struggle to establish their control at lower levels, a struggle which was far from successful by the end of the 1930s. It is misleading, however, to see the Terror as simply an attempt by the centre to assert its control over regional leaders because many figures and institutions at the centre also suffered severely from the Terror. If the Terror was directed at the regional Party apparatus, why did other bodies, including central ones, also suffer? While the regional Party figures did suffer in the Terror, they were not the only ones, which suggests that it was not purely an attempt to bring them to heel.

PROBLEMS AND ISSUES
● Role of the party

Getty's point about the lack of unity of the process from 1933 to 1939 has some validity, but is also open to question. The purge of 1933–34 and the verification and exchange were all different from the Terror of 1936–38. They were not blood purges in which people lost their lives; the purging was not carried out by an organ outside the Party (the NKVD in 1936–38); and they appear to have been organisationally more orderly and less messy than the Terror. But it is wrong to argue that they were not political but administrative. Although they were explicitly designed to repair Party administrative procedures and to root out from the Party categories of people whose qualities did not merit Party membership, many of those people were also seen as enemies. People who deceived the Party, violated its discipline, and questioned its decisions were enemies with a Party card in their pockets. They were seen not just as people who had accidentally gained Party membership, but as people who were secretly working to thwart the Party's aims. In this sense, these earlier campaigns were hunts for enemies as well as attempts to bring about organisational consolidation. Thus they added to the growing atmosphere of the search for 'enemies of the people' that was such an important part of the 1936–38 period.

What does all of this mean for an explanation of the Terror? It suggests that in their pure forms, both the orthodox and revisionist accounts need modification. Certainly Stalin wanted to get rid of those who opposed him and his policies. The Riutin Platform and the Seventeenth Congress convinced him of the need to act. The 1933–34 purge seems to have been in part an initial attempt to deal with opponents. There is no evidence of Stalin's planning of Kirov's murder, as discussed in the main text (see p.124), but it certainly served his ends. Both the verification and exchange were designed in part to remove opponents, but the effect of these was minimal. Having tried to eliminate opposition through the normal Party channels (purge, verification and exchange) and failed, Stalin now turned to the gun. The Terror achieved his end of consolidating control and eliminating opposition. This explanation does not assume that Stalin had a clear plan, but it does assume that he was a major actor in the whole process. He was not the only actor; it was in the interests of other political leaders at the centre to strengthen central controls over regional Party organisations, so this fitted in well with the political aim of reducing opposition from the lower levels. This sort of explanation thus sees the Terror not as the result of a carefully laid out plan, but of a combination of individual and group interests at the top.

Extent of the Terror

There has also been debate about the extent of the Terror. The orthodox interpretation tends to adopt very high casualty figures, like those cited in the main text (see p.127). It also assumes that the Terror affected all sections of society and that fear was present at all levels and in all areas. But these figures have recently come under question.

In an increasingly bitter debate, a number of Western students have challenged these high casualty figures. According to Stephen Wheatcroft, in 1939 there were at most three to four million people in labour camps (cf. ten to 12 million by Conquest), about 200 000 Party members were arrested and presumably shot (cf. Conquest's one million plus), and that 'excess deaths' during the Terror numbered about one million. Chris Ward reports KGB figures that the numbers in the camps were as follows: 1934 510 307; 1935 965 742; 1936 1 296 494; 1937 1 196 369; 1938 1 881 570; 1939 1 677 438. These figures take no account of deaths and imprisonment in institutions other than the camps.

This impression of a lower level impact of the Terror is reinforced by the work of Robert Thurston. Thurston acknowledges that large numbers of people were caught up in the Terror, including many innocent people. However, he argues that there was no general climate of fear in the Soviet Union during the 1930s; that the populace as a whole did not feel terrorised even though certain groups may have suffered in this way; and that many who remained untouched by the Terror did not see themselves as potential victims but believed that those arrested must have been guilty. This view suggests that the sort of social paralysis which Conquest sees as flowing from the mass scale of the Terror could not have happened, otherwise society would have collapsed.

There is no way of ever conclusively resolving this issue of the scale of the Terror. Accurate figures are unlikely to be found. Memoir material is valuable for giving a sense of an individual's perspective but (unless it is the memoir of someone in a position with access to the broader picture, which is unlikely) cannot give an accurate sense of scale, and the memory of survivors is notoriously defective. There clearly is a difference in scale between the orthodox and revisionist views. Conquest's figures seem very high and, simply in terms of the society continuing to function, it is likely that the lower figures are closer to the actual situation. But even if these lower figures are accepted as within the range, the scale of the Terror was large. Although the census figures are in dispute, if the population at the end of the 1930s was some 194 million, and if we accept the Wheatcroft figures cited above, there may still have been as much as two per cent of the population caught up in the Terror. This is a significant section of society, particularly when it is likely to have fallen hardest in the urban areas.

In sum, the debate about the Terror will continue, but neither the orthodox nor the revisionist position should be accepted without question.

List of references

Christian, David, 'History, Myth and the Stalinist Purges', *Teaching History* 22:3, October 1988.

Conquest, Robert, *The Great Terror*, Penguin, Harmondsworth, 1971 (originally published in 1968). Also *The Great Terror: A Reassessment*, Oxford University Press, Oxford, 1990.

Getty, J. Arch, *Origins of the Great Purges. The Soviet Communist Party Reconsidered, 1933–1938*, Cambridge University Press, Cambridge, 1985.

—— 'Party and purge in Smolensk: 1933–37', *Slavic Review* 42:1, 1983.

Gill, Graeme, *The Origins of the Stalinist Political System*, Cambridge University Press, Cambridge, 1990.

Khrushchev, N.S., 'On the Cult of Personality and Its Consequences', in T.H. Rigby (ed.), *The Stalin Dictatorship*, Sydney University Press, Sydney, 1968.

Medvedev, Roy, *Let History Judge. The Origins and Consequences of Stalinism*, Oxford University Press, Oxford, 1989 (originally published in English in 1972, in Russian in 1971).

Rittersporn, Gabor Tamas, *Stalinist Simplifications and Soviet Complications: Social Tensions and Political Conflicts in the USSR 1933–1953*, Harwood Academic Publishers, Reading, 1991 (originally published in French in 1988).

Schapiro, Leonard, *The Communist Party of the Soviet Union*, Methuen, London, 1970 (originally published 1963).

Thurston, R.W., 'Fear and Belief in the USSR's "Great Terror": Response to Arrest, 1935–39' *Slavic Review* 45:2, 1986.

Tucker, Robert C., *Stalin in Power. The Revolution from Above, 1928–1941*, W.W. Norton & Co, New York, 1990.

Ward, Chris, *Stalin's Russia*, Edward Arnold, London, 1993.

For the debate on casualties, see S. Rosefielde, 'An Assessment of the Sources and Uses of Gulag Forced Labour, 1929–56', *Soviet Studies* 33:1, 1981; S.G. Wheatcroft, 'On Assessing the Size of Forced Concentration Camp Labour in the Soviet Union, 1931–56', *Soviet Studies* 33:2, 1981; R. Conquest, 'Forced Labour Statistics: Some Comments', *Soviet Studies* 35:3, 1982; S. Wheatcroft, 'Towards a Thorough Analysis of Soviet Forced Labour Statistics', *Soviet Studies* 35:2, 1983; S.G. Wheatcroft, 'New Demographic Evidence on Excess Collectivization Deaths: Yet another kliuvka from Steven Rosefielde?', *Slavic Review* 44:3, 1985; B.A. Anderson & R.D. Silver, 'Demographic Analysis and Population Catastrophes in the USSR', *Slavic Review* 44:3, 1985; B.A. Anderson & R.D. Silver, 'Tautologies in the Study of Excess Mortality in the USSR in the 1930s', *Slavic Review* 45:2, 1986; S. Rosefielde, 'Incriminating Evidence: excess deaths and forced labour under Stalin: a final reply to critics', *Soviet Studies* 39:2, 1987; E. Bacon, '"Glasnost" and the Gulag: new information on Soviet forced labour around World War II', *Soviet Studies* 44:6, 1992.

Essay Questions

1 Explain the methods used by Stalin in his steady rise to a position of undisputed dominance, with reference to the period 1924 to the late 1930s.

2 Explain how the concept of counter-revolution was employed by the Soviet leadership to justify many of their actions during the 1920s and 1930s.

3 Was the development of a dictatorial regime relying heavily on the use of terror a natural consequence of the Bolshevik seizure of power?

4 '...We are fifty to a hundred years behind the advanced countries. We must cover this distance in ten years. Either we do this or they will crush us' (from a speech by Stalin to industrial managers in February 1931). Explain how Stalin went about achieving this objective and evaluate his success.

5 EITHER 'a revolutionary whose concern was to consolidate the achievements of Lenin'; OR 'a dictator simply intent upon the accumulation of more and more power': which is the more accurate description of the Stalin of the 1930s?

THE WAR AND LATE STALINISM

THE GREATEST CHALLENGE the Soviet system faced before the 1980s was that posed by the German invasion in 1941. The system came through that challenge, but the costs were enormous. The cult of Stalin continued to be all-pervasive, with the attendant stifling of creativity and cultural uniformity.

Focus questions

The following questions provide a focus for study of this era:

- How prepared was the USSR for World War II?
- What changes did the war bring to the structuring of supreme power in the USSR?
- What effect did the war have on the symbolism of the regime?
- How important was Stalin to the Soviet war effort?
- How was Stalin able to retain his absolute authority in the post-war period?

During the 1930s, the question of power in the USSR had been decided decisively in favour of the Party; both countryside and city had been brought under Party control in the upheavals at the start of the decade. Within the Party, the questions of power and authority had also been settled, in favour of the personal dominance of Stalin. As the 1930s drew to a close, however, a new challenge was appearing in the form of an expansionist Germany. In 1941, that challenge became direct and immediate.

GERMAN INVASION

PROBLEMS
AND ISSUES
● Communism and
  the 'Great
  Patriotic War'
● Modernisation

When German forces invaded the Soviet Union on the night of 21–22 June 1941, Stalin was caught by surprise. He had disregarded warnings of impending German attack given to him by Soviet sources in both Germany and Japan and by the British government. Evidence available to those at the front was also ignored: the departure of German ships from Soviet ports, the overflight of Soviet territory by German planes photographing the landscape, and the build-up of German forces near the Soviet border. Stalin's ignoring of these warnings is difficult to understand. While scepticism about the information coming from Churchill may have been justified by his anti-Bolshevism and the belief that Britain wanted to break up the Nazi–Soviet Pact and bring the USSR into the war on the anti-German side, why Stalin should ignore the evidence of his own agents is puzzling. In any event, this proved to be a costly mistake.

The main value to the Soviet Union of the Nazi–Soviet Pact should have been the breathing space it provided for the Soviet leadership to increase its military preparations. But by the time of the invasion, little concerted effort had been made to place the country on a war footing. Although the Soviet industrialisation effort was very impressive, it had not been directed overwhelmingly at the production of military equipment. This had been changing prior to the German attack, as Table 6.1 shows:

Table 6.1 Proportion of Budget Devoted to Defence

Alec Nove, *An Economic History of the USSR*, Penguin, Harmondsworth, 1982, pp.228–9

1933	3.4%
1937	16.5%
1940	32.6%

The economy was not geared for imminent war in 1941, with the result that when war broke out, deficiencies in equipment (both quality and quantity) were evident. This was soon rectified, but the effects of such shortcomings on early Soviet defeats should be noted. The effects of the problems with supply were reinforced by the effects of the Terror. The purging of the military leadership and their replacement with less experienced people produced a degree of uncertainty at the top of the military structure. Many of those rapidly promoted were clearly inadequate for the tasks thrust upon them in 1941. Some had no experience of modern military command, some were Civil War leaders brought out of retirement to head sections of the military. Their shortcomings were such that numerous military leaders who had been sent to prison or the camps during the Terror were brought back directly to leadership posts in the armed forces.

PROBLEMS
AND ISSUES
● Stalinism as
  totalitarianism
● Ideology

The fighting capacity of the Soviet military was also adversely affected by deficiencies in training. Many pilots and tank commanders were sent into combat with little experience in handling their machines. Furthermore, the preparation of the military was probably hindered by the lack of an ideological or propaganda build-up to the opening of hostilities. Until the Germans attacked, the public message Soviet troops received was one of Soviet–German friendship; with the Nazi–Soviet Pact, all anti-fascist propaganda had disappeared from the Soviet press. Now Soviet soldiers were being called upon to fight their 'friends'. This sudden change can have done little for the confidence and morale of Soviet forces.

The initial German attack was disastrous for the Soviet army, and within a little over two months major German advances were made into Soviet territory. In the first attack, some thousand Soviet planes were destroyed on the ground and thousands of men were taken prisoner or killed. The Red Army was in retreat as German forces advanced on a wide front. By the end of August 1941, Leningrad was being directly threatened, the German army was more than halfway to Moscow and Kiev was in imminent danger of falling.

MOTHERLAND AND NATIONALISM: THE SOVIET RESPONSE

The reaction in Moscow to the German attack was unusual. It was Molotov, the foreign minister, who announced the opening of hostilities on Soviet radio; Stalin was neither seen nor heard in public for 11 days. It has been claimed that Stalin had panicked and was suffering from acute depression, but more recently it has been argued that at this time he was active in organising the war effort, but out of the public eye. Whatever the reason, his silence was remarkable in the light of his political dominance and the way his image projected through his cult pervaded all of society. On 3 July Stalin addressed his people. The tone he adopted was significant:

> Comrades, citizens, brothers and sisters, men of our Army and Navy! It is to you I am speaking dear friends!
>
> The perfidious military attack by Hitlerite Germany on our Motherland, begun on 22 June, is continuing...
>
> What is required to put an end to the danger imperilling our country, and what measures must be taken to crush the enemy?
>
> Above all it is essential that our people, Soviet people, should appreciate the full immensity of the danger that threatens our country, and should give up all complacency, casualness and the mentality of peaceful constructive work that was so natural before the war, but which is fatal today, when war has radically changed the whole situation. The enemy is cruel and implacable. He is out to seize our grain and oil secured by the labour of our hands. He is out to restore the rule of the landlords, to restore tsarism, to destroy the national culture and the national existence as states of the Russians, Ukrainians, Belorussians, Lithuanians, Latvians, Estonians, Uzbeks, Tatars, Moldavians, Georgians, Armenians, Azerbaijians and the other free peoples of the Soviet Union, to Germanise them, to turn them into the slaves of German princes and barons. Thus the issue is one of

T.H. Rigby (ed.), *Stalin*, Prentice Hall, Englewood Cliffs, 1966, pp.48–50

life and death for the Soviet State, of life and death for the people of the USSR; the issue is whether the peoples of the Soviet Union shall be free or fall into slavery... **99**

In a speech without the symbolism and rhetoric of the building of socialism, of Marxism and the cult, Stalin spelled out in clear and simple language the dangers confronting the Soviet Union and its populace. It was a struggle for freedom against the Germans who wished to enslave the peoples of the USSR and destroy their cultures. The people were called upon to pursue a scorched earth policy of total opposition to the invaders.

This anti-ideological tone was reinforced by Stalin's speech on the anniversary of the Revolution, 7 November 1941. In this address he appealed to Russian patriotism, linking the current struggle with military heroes of the Russian past, Alexander Nevsky, Dmitri Donskoi, Suvorov and Kutuzov. These were the military leaders in the struggles against, respectively, the Teutonic Knights in the thirteenth century, the Tartars in the fourteenth century, the Turks and Poles in the eighteenth century, and Napoleon in the nineteenth century.

PROBLEMS AND ISSUES

- The 'Great Patriotic War'
- Ideology

The Great Patriotic War

The level of patriotic and nationalistic propaganda increased greatly with the war. While nationalism had been becoming increasingly prominent in the public images of the 1930s, it took the war to make it the dominant image. The building of the Russian state and its defence against external aggression were continuing themes, both in the history books of the period and in popular culture. The church, vigorously suppressed in the 1930s, was rehabilitated and, with all of its symbolism and weight, was thrown into the anti-German struggle. Parallels between the great tsars, the defenders of the holy Russian lands, and the present were drawn; army uniforms were redesigned to resemble those of tsarist times. The symbolism of the Russian motherland was inescapable as the system reached back into the collective memory of the people to tap the nationalist identification that was embedded there. The war became the Great Patriotic War.

Such an appeal did not have universal acceptance. For many of the non-Russian nationalities in the USSR, an appeal to Great Russian history was likely to evoke hostility at Russian conquest and rule rather than patriotic fervour. Attempts were therefore made to revive that sense of nationalism among the non-Russian people that had been suppressed in the 1930s, although this nationalism was always presented as existing within a Soviet framework. Nevertheless, in many parts of Ukraine and the Baltic states, the advancing German troops were greeted as saviours. Even in regions where they were not greeted in this way, many looked upon them with some hope rather than hostility. These sorts of sentiments were particularly widespread in those areas incorporated into the Soviet Union as a result of the Nazi–Soviet Pact, but they were also common in parts of Ukraine where locally-rooted Ukrainian nationalism had managed to survive the onslaught of the 1930s.

At the outbreak of the war, patriotic themes became paramount. This 1941 poster by I. Toidze is headed 'The Motherland is summoning you!' The paper held by the woman representing the Motherland is entitled: 'The military oath' (Sovietsky Khudoznik Publishers, Moscow)

When the brutality of the Nazi treatment of the local populations became known, however, feelings changed. For many, this led to support for the Red Army in the struggle to expel the invaders. For others, it resulted in support for one of the bands of partisans that grew up behind German lines. The Party leadership in Moscow had discussed the formation of partisan forces as early as July 1941, but it was not until May 1942 that a central organisation to co-ordinate partisan activities was established. In many parts of the country people did not wait for such central direction; local partisan groups emerged in many places, especially Ukraine. Such groups were often motivated by a fierce nationalism directed against both German forces and Soviet authorities, so much so that final suppression of some of them did not occur until the 1950s. Despite what in the eyes of Moscow was questionable political loyalty, these groups often performed an important harrying role against the German armed forces.

The problem of dissident nationalism was clearly a major concern of Stalin and his colleagues. This is most clearly shown in the treatment accorded to a number of small national groupings during the war. Between October 1943 and June 1944, the Volga Germans, Crimean Tartars, Meshkhetians, Kalmyks, Chechens, Ingushi, Balkars and Karachai were accused of collaborating with the Germans and deported in their entirety from their homelands to areas of Kazakhstan and southern Siberia. While the charges were for the most part false, they reflect official consciousness of the nationality issue and the potential danger it posed during the war.

Discuss and Review

- How was the basis for Russian patriotism and reverence of pre-Revolutionary military heroes established during the 1930s?
- Compare the ideological basis of the Great Patriotic War with that of the Civil War.
- Put yourself in the position of a devoted follower of Stalin: write a paragraph in which you explain your reaction to the news of 22 June 1941 that German forces are invading Russia.

- Compare Stalin's speech of 3 July 1941 with those he had delivered previously. How do they compare? Are there any significant changes in tone, etc?
- Design an official poster aimed at encouraging Russia's civilian population to support the war effort against the Nazis.
- Put yourself in the position of a Ukrainian nationalist: write a paragraph in which you explain your feelings in December 1941 as German forces are closing in on Moscow.

POLITICAL AND ECONOMIC REORGANISATION

PROBLEMS AND ISSUES

- The 'Great Patriotic War'

Despite the initial uncertainty, the Soviet leadership moved swiftly to mount the war effort. On 30 June 1941 the established formal structure of supreme power in the USSR was recast with the formation of the State Defence Committee (GKO) headed by Stalin. This was a small body, initially consisting of five, and from February 1942 eight people, that was to exercise absolute authority and power over all Party, state, military and other organisations throughout the country. It was a civilian body, with Marshal Voroshilov the only military member, although he was soon removed from operational military command. The dominating co-ordination and organisational role played by GKO was a firm statement of the principle of civilian command over the military. The military side of the command structure was focused in the *Stavka*, or Supreme Command. This was headed by Stalin and consisted of all the marshals of the Soviet Union, the chief of the General Staff and the leaders of the various services. It was here that all military planning was to be concentrated. Co-ordination between GKO and *Stavka* was maintained through Stalin's presence on both bodies and the right of members of the former to attend meetings of the latter.

At this time, too, the economy was placed on a war footing. One of the advantages of a command economy of the type developed in the Soviet Union is that resources can quickly be diverted to meet an emergency. So it was in the war. All efforts were turned to producing war material, and although the Western allies played an important part in providing essential equipment and resources, particularly through such schemes as the US 'lend-lease' arrangement, the bulk of Soviet war needs was met through domestic production.

This poster by P. Karachentsov from 1942 reflects the mobilisation of the economy for the war effort, and more particularly the contribution made by heavy industry and metallurgy complexes in the Ural Mountains. The inscription says: 'From the Urals to the front' (Sovietsky Khudoznik Publishers, Moscow)

The focus on production for the war is shown by Table 6.2 which shows industrial production and the production of arms for the war period.

Table 6.2   Industrial and Arms Production

	Industrial Index	Arms Index
1940	100	100
1941	98	140
1942	77	186
1943	90	224
1944	104	251

Roger A. Clarke & Dubravko J.I. Matko, *Soviet Economic Facts 1917-81*, Macmillan, London, 1983, p.10

The focus of wartime production was the giant heavy industry complexes developed in the Urals area, far from the scene of fighting and immune from German attack. These were supplemented by the various industrial facilities that were dismantled at their locations in the traditional industrial areas of Ukraine and western Russia and relocated in their entirety to safer regions. Some 1523 enterprises were moved eastward in the first five months of the war. During the war as a whole, some 3500 new industrial enterprises were built. When Soviet war production got going, it outproduced the Germans and provided weapons of higher quality.

Personnel changes in the leading ranks of the armed forces were also instrumental in Soviet victory. Whenever military leaders at any level displayed signs of incompetence, they were removed, even when they had been personally close to Stalin, like Marshals Voroshilov and Budyenny (both former Civil

War commanders). Those removed were often replaced by people who showed real military talent and ability. People of proven military ability like Rokossovsky, Gorbatov and Meretskov were brought back from the labour camps to which they had been sent during the Terror. But perhaps the most important appointment of all was that of Georgii Zhukov. Zhukov took charge of the defence of the capital, played a major part in organising the Soviet defensive effort along the length of the front, and led the Soviet forces into Berlin in April 1945.

MILITARY VICTORY

PROBLEMS AND ISSUES

● The 'Great Patriotic War'

After the initial successes, German forces drove on deeply into Russia. Their advance was checked at three crucial points: Leningrad, Moscow and Stalingrad. The German army had reached Leningrad in September 1941, having met little resistance on the way. But they were unable to capture Leningrad. A siege was mounted that lasted some 900 days and involved enormous suffering for the Leningrad population. Food was scarce; pets were eaten. Disease was rife and there was constant harassment from German forces on the ground and in the air. Somewhere near a million citizens died in the siege. The feat of the Leningrad people proved an inspiration not just to their Soviet cousins but to those fighting the war everywhere.

At the same time as advancing on Leningrad, German forces thrust toward Moscow. By October 1941 they were close to the capital. It was at this point that Stalin became a symbol of vital importance. Although the capital was partly evacuated, with foreign embassies and the government moving to

Women building barricades in Leningrad during the siege (UPI/Bettmann)

Kuibyshev on the Volga, Stalin remained in the Kremlin. With the Germans approaching, on 7 November Stalin took the salute of the troops in the annual march through Red Square in celebration of the Revolution. As a symbol of strength, unity and national determination, Stalin was inspiring. At the same time, along with Zhukov, he organised the defence of Moscow. The Germans, totally unprepared for the rigours of a Russian winter and surprised by a Soviet offensive launched in December 1941, were halted between Moscow's international airport and the city itself. This event, at the end of 1941, was crucial because it meant that Moscow, the most potent symbol of Russian nationalism, was saved.

Stalingrad

The victory at Moscow was important, but it did not turn the war. German forces still advanced in the south, and by mid-August 1942 they had reached the outskirts of Stalingrad on the Volga. In some ways this was to be the most important battle of the war. Soviet forces refused to surrender the city and German forces were unable to take it. The fighting came down to hand-to-hand fighting in the streets, but what finally won the battle for the Soviet side was the tactic of encirclement they adopted. Surrounded, the German troops had little alternative but to surrender in February 1943. This victory turned the tide. Although the Germans had later successes on the Soviet front, most importantly in recapturing Kharkov in May 1943, for much of the rest of the war they were retreating before the advancing Soviet troops. Led by Zhukov — with a diversion to establish control in the Balkans and a temporary halt outside Warsaw while the Germans crushed the rising in the Warsaw ghetto — the Soviet forces marched on into Europe, finally meeting with their Western allies on the Elbe.

Victory was won, but the loss and devastation were enormous. From mid-1941, the war had been principally a Soviet–German conflict. More German troops were involved on the eastern than on the western front and the death and injury toll was much greater here. About 20 million Soviet citizens died as a result of the war, more than all of those lost by the other allies combined. Almost an entire generation of males perished. In addition, there was enormous damage and destruction to the fabric of the country: cities in ruins, factories destroyed, farms completely dislocated. The losses were irreplaceable.

Stalin as Saviour of his People

One effect of the war was to inflate Stalin's image even further. He now appeared as the symbol of national victory, the saviour of his people. Like most public images, there is some truth in this. Certainly Stalin made mistakes, and these often cost the Soviet Union dearly. For example, there was an initial lack of preparation. Stalin refused to allow armies to retreat (indeed, in some cases security forces marched into battle behind regular soldiers to shoot anyone who tried to retreat) which sometimes led to their decimation or capture (as

During the war, Stalin was presented as a great war leader. This drawing, by K. Finogenov, is entitled 'At the Front' and dates from 1941 (photo by John Freeman)

in Kiev in September 1941). Stalin's over-optimistic appraisal of Soviet strength in winter 1942 allowed an unsuccessful counter-offensive by the Germans. But Stalin also played a positive role.

The image Khrushchev sketched of Stalin planning battle strategy on a globe of the world is clearly a caricature. For the most part Stalin accepted the advice of his military advisers after the initial setbacks. He used his authority to promote men of ability in a way that perhaps only a dictator could have done. Furthermore, his leadership role, shown by remaining in Moscow throughout the darkest days and in the media campaign showing him visiting the troops, was important for national morale and confidence. Just as Churchill personified British resistance, so Stalin did for the Soviet people. His image as a great war leader, while exaggerated, was not as far from the mark for many Soviet citizens as we have often thought.

Why was the Soviet Union victorious in the Great Patriotic War? Seven factors can be suggested:

- The resources available to the Soviet war leaders were much greater than those available to Germany. Particularly important was manpower, but also significant were the vast natural resources the Soviet Union possessed.
- The command economy was able to rapidly mobilise resources and organise production to meet the challenge posed by the war.
- The commitment and sacrifice of the Soviet people was critical. The populace suffered enormously but, with the exception of those sections which

initially welcomed the Germans, their support for the war effort was unstinting.
- The German forces were unprepared for the Russian winter and for the distances involved in invading the Soviet Union.
- Assistance given to the Soviet war effort by the allies.
- The strategic problems for Germany of fighting on two fronts.
- The quality of Soviet forces and generalship.

Review

- How did Soviet symbolism change during the war? Compare it with the symbolism of other powers.

Discuss

- In a perverted sense Stalin's use of terror was justified in the long term — the discipline which it imposed upon the Russian people proved to be an enduring feature and eventually one of the crucial factors which produced the defeat of Nazi Germany.

A WORLD POWER

From the time of the German attack, the Soviet Union found itself on the side of the allied powers. The latter gave significant economic assistance to the Soviet Union, but despite the common aims and the upsurge of popular pro-Soviet feeling in the West, the relationship between the wartime allies

At the Teheran Conference of the Allies, 28 November– 1 December 1943, Roosevelt, Churchill and Stalin celebrate Churchill's 69th birthday (Camera Press)

was never close. Stalin resented what he believed was allied reluctance to open up the second front by invading France, while the Western allies, and in particular Britain, were suspicious of Soviet aims and intentions once the war was concluded. Close personal rapport was never established between the leaders despite the summit meetings in Tehran in 1943 and in Yalta and Potsdam in 1945. The basis of the wartime alliance was fear of Germany, and when that was gone, the alliance had little to sustain it.

But the war did propel Russia into the ranks of the great powers. Soviet participation in the wartime summit meetings meant that it became one of the arbiters of the post-war settlement. If prior to the war the Western powers had considered Russia an outcast, its role in the victory and its new military strength (a strength reinforced by the explosion of the atomic bomb in 1949) ensured that henceforth it could not be ignored. The Soviet Union was now recognised as a major power.

Review

- Why did the Western leaders now invite Stalin to their key meetings?
- Consider how Stalin's ideology of building socialism in one country affected the Soviet Union's response to the war.
- Why were the battles of Leningrad, Moscow and Stalingrad of symbolic importance? Were all these battles strategically important?

POST-WAR STALINISM

PROBLEMS AND ISSUES

- Stalinism as totalitarianism

Stalin's personal dominance, established in the 1930s and reinforced symbolically during the war, was not threatened during the post-war period. Indeed, his dominance was so great that the regular institutions of the Party virtually ceased to function. Party Congresses were supposed to meet at three-yearly intervals, but none met between 1939 and 1952. Only six CC plenums were convened during the same period and although the Politburo, Orgburo and Secretariat seem to have met regularly, they were strictly advisory in function. Much decision-making took place outside the formal institutions, in *ad hoc* groupings of Stalin and his cronies. All the formal institutions were of little importance beside the power resting in Stalin's hands.

One institution that was important was the security apparatus. The importance that apparatus had gained during the 1930s was not significantly eroded during the war. In the post-war period the heightened concern for national security resulting from the outbreak of the Cold War promoted the security apparatus even further. Their prominence was reflected in the high office held by security chief Lavrenty Beria who, during this time, as well as being deputy prime minister in charge of security, was a full member of the Politburo. Although there were no widespread purges like those of the 1930s, the security

Generalissimo Joseph Stalin at the peak of his power (SCR)

apparatus was busy in areas newly incorporated into the Soviet Union; in dealing with those who returned to the USSR at the end of the war, including former POWs; in the purge of Leningrad following the death of the party leader Zhdanov in 1948; and in preparing the 'Doctors' Plot' in 1952–53. It is rumoured that Stalin was planning a new purge when he died (linked with the Doctors' Plot) and that only his death prevented it from happening. But while prominent, the security apparatus was not all-powerful. It was under Stalin's control.

Stalin was the most important political force in the system. Although he did not make every decision, he could decide any issue he chose. None of the institutions in the system — Party, state, military, security apparatus, trade unions — had any real independence from Stalin and most had only very limited autonomy. They were largely instruments of the dictator, the means through which he ruled. The figure of Stalin was clearly the centrepiece around which the system turned.

RECONSTRUCTION

Considerable efforts were devoted to economic reconstruction. Little attempt was made however, to improve the lot of the populace by radically altering economic priorities to increase the production of consumer goods. The emphasis remained on heavy industry, in the belief that this was the best way to manage the enormous rebuilding required after the war and, once relations soured once again with the West, to maintain military strength. Reconstruction proceeded swiftly, with damaged facilities being rapidly restored to full productive capacity. Discipline was strengthened in the factories and tight control reasserted over the farms. High levels of pressure were asserted to increase grain deliveries to the state, a policy which contributed significantly to famine in Ukraine in 1946. Agricultural revival was also slower than industrial because many of the worst battles had taken place across the most productive land in the Soviet Union.

Table 6.3 Industrial Production

	Total		Producer Goods		Consumer Goods	
	Index	Percentage change over last year	Index	Percentage change over last year	Index	Percentage increase over last year
1940	100		100		100	
1945	92	–15.3	112	–17.6	59	9.3
1946	77	–16.3	82	–26.8	67	13.6
1947	93	20.8	101	23.2	82	22.3
1948	118	26.9	130	28.7	99	20.7
1949	141	19.5	163	25.4	107	8.1
1950	173	22.7	205	25.8	123	15.0
1951	202	16.8	239	16.6	143	16.3
1952	225	11.4	268	12.1	158	10.5
1953	252	12.0	299	11.6	177	12.0

Clarke & Matko, p.10

Table 6.4 Agricultural Production

	Total		Crops		Livestock	
	Index	Percentage change over last year	Index	Percentage change over last year	Index	Percentage increase over last year
1940	100		100		100	
1945	60	11.1	57		64	
1946	68	13.3	65	14.0	76	18.8
1947	87	27.9	91	40.0	78	2.6
1948	97	11.5	102	12.1	84	7.7
1949	99	2.1	101	–1.0	95	13.1
1950	99	0	97	–4.0	104	9.5
1951	93	–6.1	86	–11.3	110	5.8
1952	101	8.6	96	11.6	113	2.7
1953	104	3.0	96	0	124	9.7

Clarke & Matko, p.14

These tables show how agriculture was much slower to reach its pre-war level than industry, and its growth was much more erratic.

As life returned to normal following the strains imposed by the war, the people looked forward to an improvement in their immediate conditions. But improvement was slow in coming. With so much of the infrastructure of the society destroyed, including an enormous quantity of housing stock, transport facilities and productive capacity, life remained hard. It continued to be characterised by shortages and poor quality. Nevertheless, by the end of Stalin's life, living standards were improving, at least in the bigger urban areas, but this was a slow and uneven process.

Review

- Compare the course of Soviet economic
recovery with that of the major powers. How would you rate the Soviet effort?

CULTURAL LIFE

PROBLEMS AND ISSUES

- Stalinism

The basis of legitimacy remained as it had been in earlier times. The cult of Stalin saturated Soviet society to an even greater extent than it had in the 1930s, embellished by success in the Great Patriotic War. The cult was reinforced by the continued public prominence of Great Russian nationalism. The tone of this is reflected in the following passage from Stalin's victory speech:

> 66 Let me propose one more toast to you. I would like to drink a toast to the health of our Soviet people, and principally to the Russian people. I drink to the health of the Russian people because it is the outstanding nation amongst all nations of the Soviet Union. I drink the toast because not only is the Russian nation the leading nation but its people show a sharp intellect, character and perseverance. 99

Pravda, 25 May 1945

Propaganda continued to emphasise the benefits the non-Russian nationalities had gained through their association with the Russians; the advances made by the former were almost always attributed to the influence and guidance of the latter. This message struck strong roots among the Great Russian people, but for the other national groups it was likely to have little attraction.

The conservatism of this nationalist appeal was matched in the cultural sphere by a consolidation of control and the reaffirmation of the principle that literature and art should serve the purposes of the construction of socialism. Culture had an aim: to contribute to the building of a bright new future. Anything which did not contribute to that aim, and therefore did not accord with the principles of 'socialist realism', did not find official favour and was unlikely to get an airing. This is clearly reflected in the famous decision published in August 1946 attacking the journals *Zvezda* and *Leningrad*:

> " The leading workers on these journals, and primarily their editors, comrades Saianov and Likharev, have forgotten the Leninist doctrine that our journals, whether scientific or artistic, cannot be apolitical. They have forgotten that our journals are a powerful instrument of the Soviet state for educating Soviet people, the youth in particular, and must therefore be guided by that which constitutes the living foundation of the Soviet order — its politics. The Soviet order cannot tolerate its youth being educated in a spirit of indifference to Soviet politics, in a 'don't give a damn' moral vacuum.
>
> The strength of Soviet literature, the most progressive literature in the world, is that it has no other interests, and cannot have any other interests than the interests of the people, the interests of the state. The task of Soviet literature is to help the state educate the youth correctly, answer its inquiries, train the new generation to be bold, to believe in its cause and not to fear obstacles, to be ready to overcome any obstacles.
>
> Therefore any doctrine which is devoid of moral content and apolitical, any 'art for art's sake', is alien to Soviet literature, is damaging to the interests of the Soviet people and State, and should have no place in our journals. "

'On the Journals *Zvezda and Leningrad*, 14 August 1946, *Resolutions and Decisions of the Communist Party*, Vol.3, pp.241–2

The result was a stifling of individual creativity and the existence of cultural uniformity. Experimentation remained subordinated to orthodoxy which ruled in all spheres of intellectual and artistic endeavour. Experimentation was also frowned upon in the social spheres. Continued emphasis on the family with measures discouraging sexual freedom, divorce and abortion accorded well with the official emphasis on status, rank, hierarchy and differentiation. Soviet society became very status conscious. Anti-semitism was also prominent. The whole public code characteristic of late Stalinism was one of propriety and what could almost be called Victorian values.

THE INTERNATIONAL CONTEXT

The emergence of the Soviet Union as a great power has already been noted. But the changed context of its existence should be recognised. Prior to 1941, the Soviet Union had been the only socialist state on the globe, with the exception of the insignificant Mongolian People's Republic. After the war, it was joined by the band of states in Eastern Europe, in 1948 by North Korea and in 1949 by China. The new states of Eastern Europe, with the exception of Yugoslavia and Albania, were all established with significant involvement by Soviet forces and were under effective Soviet control. Yugoslavia sharply broke away from Soviet control in 1948, but the Eastern European states remained satellites of the Soviet Union throughout the Stalin period. Their internal affairs were structured along Stalinist lines, even to the extent of conducting show trials in the late 1940s and early 1950s, and their foreign policies were largely directed from Moscow. Only Yugoslavia was able to escape this fate, and even though this dented Stalin's prestige and was of considerable annoyance to him, it did not alter the basic political fact: the Soviet Union now had a defensive buffer between itself and its chief potential source of attack.

The gains made as a result of the extension of Soviet control over Eastern Europe were offset by the deterioration in relations between the Soviet Union and its wartime allies. Western fears about Soviet expansionism reinforced the pre-war concerns about the nature of the regime, and led to growing hostility towards the USSR. Relations became strained in 1946, reflected in Churchill's speech in Fulton, Missouri, where he declared that 'an iron curtain has descended across the Continent'. These strains were intensified at the end of the 1940s by the Berlin crisis, the Soviet explosion of an atomic bomb and Chinese Communist victory, all in 1949, and the Korean War in 1950. The so-called 'Cold War' had begun, and with it a return to an arms build up. The insecurity that had been present in the 1920s and 1930s returned, and as in the former period, it provided the rationale for the tightening of domestic discipline noted above.

It was at this time, with heightened internal tension and a domestic emphasis on discipline and internal enemies (in the form of the Doctors' Plot), that Stalin died, on 5 March 1953.

Discuss

- Discuss the effect of the war on the Soviet Union's international position.
- Discuss the relationship between economic reconstruction, cultural conservatism and international hostility. Is this a recurring theme in Soviet history?

CASE STUDY 6

Was the Stalin Regime Totalitarian?

In the period following World War II, many observers were struck by the similarities they saw between Nazi Germany and the Stalinist Soviet Union. In an attempt to find some means of understanding the dynamics of these regimes, the notion of *totalitarianism* was suggested by a number of scholars. The first large-scale attempt to use the term in an analytical fashion was by Hannah Arendt, but the most important systematic attempt to apply it to the Soviet Union came in the work of Carl Friedrich and Zbigniew Brzezinski, published in 1956. Publications mentioned are listed at the end.

Definitions of Totalitarianism

According to Friedrich and Brzezinski, a totalitarian system was qualitatively different from all other types of systems, and consisted of a 'cluster of traits', all of which had to be present for a totalitarian system to exist. The traits were:

- 'An elaborate ideology, consisting of an official body of doctrine covering all vital aspects of man's existence to which everyone living in that society is supposed to adhere, at least passively.' The ideology is directed towards a perfect final state.
- A single mass party which is hierarchically and oligarchically organised and typically led by one man, 'the dictator'. The mass party consists of a relatively small percentage of the population and is either superior to or intertwined with the governmental bureaucracy.
- 'A system of terror, whether physical or psychic, effected through party and secret-police control, supporting but also supervising the party for its leaders, and characteristically directed not only against demonstrable "enemies" of the regime, but against more or less arbitrarily selected classes of the population.'
- 'A technologically conditioned, near-complete monopoly of control, in the hands of the party and of the government, of all means of effective mass communication, such as the press, radio, and motion pictures.'
- 'A similarly technologically conditioned, near-complete monopoly of the effective use of all weapons of armed combat.'
- 'A central control and direction of the entire economy through the bureaucratic co-ordination of formerly independent corporate entities, typically including most other associations and group activities.'

Carl J. Friedrich & Zbigniew K. Brzezinski, *Totalitarian Dictatorship and Autocracy*, Harvard University Press, Cambridge (Mass), 1956, p.22

One problem with this cluster of traits for those who wanted to use the totalitarian model to analyse the post-Stalin USSR was that following Stalin's death, the system of terror was dismantled. The original model therefore appeared no longer applicable. In response, in the second edition, Friedrich amended this checklist by arguing that what was necessary was that terror was always present as a last resort, and that the absence of criticism showed the presence of terror. He thus substituted a notion of 'internalised terror' for the overt terror system of the original model.

Not all theorists of totalitarianism have used the Friedrich-Brzezinski approach. Arendt focused upon the 'essence' of totalitarianism, which she saw to be the atomisation of society. She argued that control was so extensive and diverse in the forms it took that all notion of a private sphere was broken down. Leonard Schapiro produced a model consisting of contours (personal rule, subjugation of the legal order, control over private morality, and mobilisation and mass legitimacy) and instruments of rule (ideology, party, and control by the leader's apparatus). Others have adopted slightly different approaches to these, but all have as an essential component the extensive control over all areas of life by the regime.

Applying the Model

In seeking to evaluate the appropriateness of the term totalitarian to Stalin's Soviet Union, the original Friedrich-Brzezinski model is best used because it was this model which was both specifically designed to apply to the USSR and which set the tone for later studies. Its appropriateness will be evaluated by looking at each of the six points in turn.

The elaborate ideology: Throughout the Stalin period, the Soviet regime did project an elaborate ideology, Marxism-Leninism. This was based on the writing of Marx, Engels and Lenin, 'creatively developed' by Stalin and his professional ideologues. The ideology sought to embrace all aspects of life, it laid down the boundaries within which discussion and intellectual development could occur, and it was projected widely through the press. In this sense it was a crucial control mechanism for the regime. All were expected to adhere to it, and publicly most did.

A single mass party: The Communist Party throughout the Stalin period was one of the main institutions in the system and, prior to the Terror, the most important body. It was organised hierarchically and oligarchically, and it was led by a single leader. While it had a mass membership, that membership constituted a small percentage of the population. The Party was fully intertwined with other organisational structures in the society, including the state apparatus. It was through such intertwining that the Party was a means of control.

A system of terror: From 1936 a system of terror did exist in the sense that the security apparatus could arrest people virtually at will. There were no clear institutional barriers to its activity and little effective defence against it for the populace. In the late 1930s, not even Party membership was protection against being arrested. This meant that terroristic control seemed highly arbitrary.

Near-complete monopoly of control over mass communications: All means of mass communications were in official hands and, through an extensive system of censorship, ensured that a fairly standard message was projected onto society. There was no right to independent publication, and any attempt to do so was crushed.

Near-complete monopoly of weapons of armed combat: Apart from some dissident nationalist groups, especially in Estonia and Ukraine following the war, the regime monopolised weapons.

Central control and direction of the economy: This was achieved through the integration of economic organs into the overall politico-administrative structure of control directed principally through the Party. The command economy which was established at the end of the 1920s virtually eliminated the private sector from the economy. Although private activity was able to reappear in the guise of private plots and through the black market, the basic economic structure remained under state control.

Restrictions on Central Control

It seems that all six traits identified by Friedrich and Brzezinski were realised to a significant degree in Stalin's USSR. One reservation must be registered, however, and this concerns the extent of control. The notion of totalitarianism entails wide-ranging control by the centre of virtually all aspects of life in the society. It is the extent of this control that distinguishes the totalitarian system from all other types of political system. The problem is that in the conditions which prevailed in Stalin's USSR, the conditions did not exist which would enable such tight control to be implemented. There are two aspects to this.

Firstly, studies have shown (Getty, Gill) that during the 1930s the Communist Party was not a highly centralised and disciplined organisation. Although decision-making was highly concentrated in Stalin and the people immediately around him, the relationship between the centre and regional Party organs was very much weaker than many people have thought. Because of inadequate channels of communication, underdeveloped machinery for conducting Party internal business, and the poor state of internal Party record-keeping, the centre often did not have very much idea about what was happening at lower levels. Lower level leaders often ignored central instructions without suffering any penalty. Certainly when it wished the centre could intervene and remove local leaders, but it could not exercise continuing close control. This sort of situation continued after the war and prevailed until at least the time of Stalin's death. In this sense, the Party was much more loosely organised than would be consistent with the totalitarian model.

Secondly, throughout this period the Soviet Union suffered from an inadequate communications network. Parts of the country were not well served by radio, telephone, mail and transport systems, with the result that central control over these parts of the country was not as tight as the centre may have wished. It was the inadequacy of such mechanisms of control that increased the importance of ideology as a means of tying people to central commands. But these technical limitations were a barrier to the exercise of effective central control in all parts of the country.

These restrictions on tight central control pose real limits to the applicability of the totalitarian model to the Soviet Union. Clearly if the central politico-administrative apparatus had limited ability to exercise control throughout the country, it does not meet the criterion of high level of control, which is the essence of totalitarianism. But this does not make the notion of totalitarianism irrelevant. If the Soviet centre had the highest degree of control possible given the limits of technology and of geography, one can argue that Stalin's USSR meets the criteria for totalitarianism to a significant degree. Indeed, it may be the case that the USSR came closer to the totalitarian ideal than any other contemporary political system. Thus while it did not fully meet the demands of the totalitarian model, the Stalinist regime may have been the closest approximation to it at the time.

List of references

Arendt, Hannah, *The Origins of Totalitarianism*, Andre Deutsch, London, 1986 (originally published 1951).

Friedrich, Carl J. & Brzezinski, Zbigniew K., *Totalitarian Dictatorship and Autocracy*, Harvard University Press, Cambridge (Mass), 1956 (second edition revised by Friedrich, 1965).

Getty, J. Arch, *Origins of the Great Purges. The Soviet Communist Party Reconsidered, 1933–1938*, Cambridge University Press, Cambridge, 1985.

Gill, Graeme, *The Origins of the Stalinist Political System*, Cambridge University Press, Cambridge, 1990.

Schapiro, Leonard, *Totalitarianism*, Macmillan, London, 1972.

Essay Questions

1 How did Stalin's use of ideology change with circumstances?

2 'If it had not been for the foresight and drive of Stalin during the 1930s Russia would not even have been in a position to resist, let alone defeat, Nazi Germany in the 1940s.' Is this a valid assessment?

3 Did Stalin establish a totalitarian regime?

4 'With the passing of time bureaucratic control, rather than the implementation of ideological goals, became more and more the guiding principle of Russia's Communist Party.' How valid is this assessment?

THE FATE OF THE REVOLUTION

THE FATE of the October Revolution has been a question of concern to scholars and political activists since at least 1921. Some of the opposition to NEP was based on the belief that it betrayed the socialist ideals for which the Revolution was fought. The emergence of Stalin and the dictatorial and coercive regime he headed raised the question of whether the Revolution itself was responsible for giving birth to such a regime, or was its emergence an accidental development. This question was of particular concern to people

The USSR after World War II

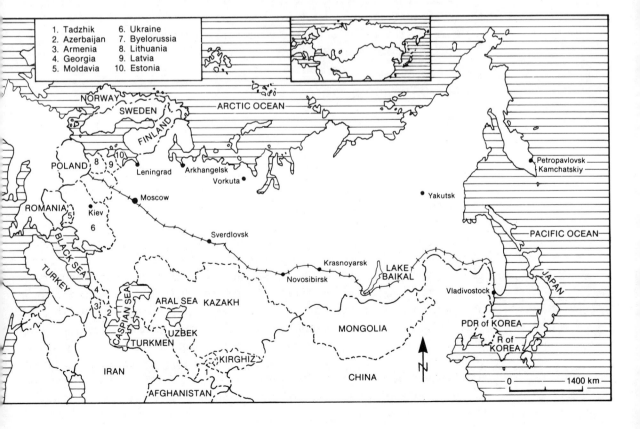

1. Tadzhik
2. Azerbaijan
3. Armenia
4. Georgia
5. Moldavia
6. Ukraine
7. Byelorussia
8. Lithuania
9. Latvia
10. Estonia

NORWAY
SWEDEN
FINLAND
ARCTIC OCEAN
POLAND
Leningrad
Arkhangelsk
Vorkuta
Petropavlovsk Kamchatskiy
Moscow
ROMANIA
Kiev
Yakutsk
Sverdlovsk
PACIFIC OCEAN
Krasnoyarsk
LAKE BAIKAL
TURKEY
BLACK SEA
Novosibirsk
Vladivostock
JAPAN
CASPIAN SEA
ARAL SEA
KAZAKH
UZBEK
TURKMEN
MONGOLIA
PDR of KOREA
R of KOREA
KIRGHIZ
IRAN
CHINA
N
AFGHANISTAN
0   1400 km

on the left of the political spectrum, with Trotsky perhaps the first to raise
the question in these terms. The collapse of the USSR in 1991 raised the same
question in a slightly different form: was the whole Soviet experience a failure?
These questions are the focus of this Epilogue.

AIMS AND ACHIEVEMENTS

The aims of the Revolution, as reflected in the aspirations of its makers and
in the early statements of the new regime, were highly laudable. Lenin and
his colleagues wanted to establish a socialist society characterised by freedom,
equality and peace. Certainly this was the public message they presented, and
although some have argued that Lenin in particular was motivated purely by
a drive for power, it is unlikely that this alone could have sustained the
Bolshevik elite through the hardships they had to endure before gaining power.
In difficult times, people are sustained by ideals, and it would be churlish
to deny the commitment to ideals within the ranks of the Bolshevik elite.

The achievements of the October Revolution fell somewhat short of these
lofty ideals, at least in the form in which the latter frequently were expressed.
Soviet reality fell far short of the picture of society sketched in Lenin's *The
State and Revolution*, where freedom, equality and the populace as a whole
play a direct part in administration and governance. But this does not mean
that these aims are completely irrelevant to an evaluation of the Soviet experience. By the 1970s, society was probably more equal and, in one sense,
freer than it had been in 1917.

Equality in Society

The key to greater equality was the massive economic development set in
train at the end of the 1920s. By propelling large parts of the population into
the newly developed economic structures (factories, collective farms); by controlling the incomes they could gain through such employment; and by almost
eliminating the effects of inherited wealth through wholesale expropriation
of wealth at the time of the Revolution, the state was able to shape the social
structure of Soviet society. When wage equalisation policies were pursued
in the 1960s and 1970s, their effects in creating social equality were significant.
By the early 1970s, wage differentials (the gap between highest paid and lowest
paid) were lower in the USSR than in any other highly industrialised country.

This does not mean that there was real equality. Privileges, in the form
of increased non-wage payments, access to scarce commodities, health care,
holidays and so on, were available on a differential scale to certain sections
of the populace, especially those at the higher levels of the politico-
administrative structure. Access to such goods was highly unequal and clearly
undermined the Soviet claim for an equal society. The ability of some sections
of the population to generate income through private activity, particularly

on the black market, was another factor undercutting claims for equality.

Nevertheless, certain aspects of Soviet development policies had a significant positive effect on the standing of the Soviet people. By the late 1960s–early 1970s, living standards had risen remarkably; the current Soviet generation of 20–30 year olds could look at their own standards of living and see that they were higher than those of their parents. Government subsidies on food, accommodation, power and transport greatly reduced the amount ordinary Soviet citizens had to spend on these items. An extensive welfare net, including medical services and a range of pension entitlements, and a full employment policy took considerable uncertainty out of the lives of Soviet citizens. (This is the sense in which Soviet citizens may be considered freer than their pre-1917 forebears — the fear of economic deprivation was less and therefore the capacity to act was less inhibited by such concerns.) Education was free and universal, thereby opening up a major channel of social mobility to all.

Costs of economic development

It is clear that major advances had been achieved in the economic and social sphere within a relatively short space of time. Within a couple of generations, the Soviet Union had been transformed from a primarily agricultural country into one of the world's superpowers. Its population had become mainly urbanised, well educated, and enjoyed generally higher standards of living than those of any time in the past. But this progress was not without costs. A number of costs can be identified:

The enormous loss of life: Even leaving aside the casualties during the war, which may have been increased by the regime's failure adequately to prepare but which would probably have occurred in any case, the human cost of Soviet economic development was enormous. Exact totals are impossible to obtain, but combining approximations for the toll of collectivisation and the Terror produces a figure that may be as high as 35 million people. To this must be added those who perished in the initial years of Soviet rule, during World War II as a result of regime actions (such as the deportation of national groups) and in the post-war period. Even for social engineering conducted for the most laudable of aims, this is an unacceptably high cost.

Lack of freedom: From 1917 until 1989, the Soviet populace had no effective say in who was to rule them. Although the Soviet regime provided numerous institutional means through which the populace could be consulted, there was no provision for a popular veto over policy or personnel. Furthermore, the activities of the security apparatus ensured that oppositional activity was likely to be met with unacceptable consequences. Press censorship and media control made freedom of speech impossible, while strict passport controls closely monitored the movement of citizens inside the USSR. The fact that the state was virtually the only employer also discouraged dissidence. Such controls were not totally effective in snuffing out dissident thought or activity, but they did have considerable success in this.

Lack of initiative: The sort of society which tried to prevent any dissidence while at the same time providing for all of its citizens' needs produced a citizenry characterised by apathy and a lack of initiative, at least in the public sphere. In their public life citizens were usually more than willing to accept instructions, to do their jobs adequately and not to rock the boat either by taking up a dissident stance or by suggesting ways in which current procedures could be improved. Life became increasingly privatised, as people only showed their true feelings to trusted friends and family members. The degree to which this public docility had taken hold was evident in the contrast that emerged in the last years of the Soviet regime's life when the people took to the streets in large numbers to press for change. This activity highlighted the absence of such a public role for the populace during the Soviet period.

Low standards: The principal measure of success used by Soviet authorities in evaluating economic performance was gross output. Little attention was given to the quality of the goods produced, except in the defence sector. This was particularly the case in the production of consumer goods. As a result, the standard of goods produced was often poor. Appliances that did not work, clothes that were ill-fitting and housing that was cramped and poorly constructed were the subject of frequent complaint. But because there were no alternative sources of supply, the consumer had to accept what was produced. Furthermore, the priority given to heavy industry over light industry meant that even these poor quality consumer goods were in short supply. This meant that citizens for much of the Soviet period lived in a state of bare sufficiency. While living standards were therefore better in the 1960s and 1970s than they had been earlier, they were significantly lower than in most industrialised states, and life remained hard for many people.

Environmental degradation: The low standards of most goods produced were matched by low standards in environmental protection. The push to industrialise rapidly at any cost meant that no attempt was made to protect the environment against degradation caused by such development. In the short term, even where there were environmental safeguards that could be built into factories, they were usually not included because of the extra cost they involved. The result has been that parts of the Soviet Union have suffered from environmental degradation and destruction on a large scale: rivers and lakes are polluted (the Aral Sea is even disappearing as a result of excessive irrigation); soil and sub-soil are degraded by contaminants; pristine forests have been chopped down or affected by acid rain; some areas have been rendered radioactive by nuclear accidents. Environmental costs are enormous.

These costs are all significant. How they are to be measured against the achievements is unclear and a matter of some debate. Both costs and achievements have been real, but both defy accurate measurement. What is clear is that both were the result of the course of development pursued by the Stalinist regime. This raises the question of the relationship between the October Revolution and the Stalinist regime.

OCTOBER, LENIN AND STALIN

Many people on the left of the political spectrum have pointed to the ideals of October and the realities of the Stalin regime and asked how the one could have led to the other. Many on the right have been willing to argue that October and the regime established by Lenin inevitably led to the coercive, terrorist regime of Stalin. But is this a fair explanation?

Three basic types of explanation have been offered for the emergence of the Stalinist regime.

Essentialist: This is the view that Stalinism is the expression or realisation of the essence of some other historical force. Two main historical forces have been suggested: Leninism, or the type of system established immediately following the October Revolution; and bureaucracy. The nucleus of the argument about the relationship between Leninism and Stalinism is that the political and organisational principles and prejudices on which the Soviet Union was established under Lenin inevitably led to the type of political system led by Stalin. It is argued that the organisational structure sketched in Lenin's *What is to be Done?* allied to the elimination of all opposition led to a centralised structure with no acceptance of diversity, the Red Terror laid the foundations for the Great Terror of the 1930s, and Lenin's personal dictatorship led to Stalin's personal dictatorship. This is popularly called the 'continuity thesis'. (This is discussed at length in Stephen F. Cohen, 'Bolshevism and Stalinism', in Robert C. Tucker (ed.), *Stalinism. Essays in Historical Interpretation*, Princeton University Press, Princeton, 1977).

The argument about bureaucracy as the social force of Stalinism was first put forward by Leon Trotsky. This view sees Stalin as merely the representative of the bureaucracy which, through its control over information and its political power, was able to push the democrats out of power in the early years of the Soviet regime and establish its own control. The regime's need to administer the society it had conquered paved the way for bureaucratic dominance and this lifted Stalin to his position of power.

Contextual: This argument focuses on the context within which the Bolshevik regime came to power. Its nucleus is the argument that the combination of Russian backwardness and the isolation of the Revolution led to a centralist, dictatorial regime. Economic backwardness could be overcome quickest by a centralised economic system, while the establishment of political centralism was the best defence against opposition, both external and internal. This argument sees the Stalinist regime as a response to the difficulties and dangers involved in building socialism in an underdeveloped country.

Personalist: This argument sees the main reason for the emergence of the Stalinist regime to be Stalin himself. His personality and drive for power are seen as the principal factors shaping the emergence of a dictatorial power system. It is sometimes argued that Stalin suffered from a major inferiority complex, and that his life was devoted to building up his personal ego through the acquisition of supreme and unlimited power. Whether this psychological portrait of Stalin is accepted or not, the basis of the personalist explanation is not demolished: the principal cause of the structuring of the regime is Stalin's drive for power.

All three explanations have their supporters, but all three are flawed. The principal problem with the essentialist argument is exactly the reverse of the problem with the personalist explanation. The essentialist argument gives sole responsibility to the operation of inanimate historical forces, the essence of Leninism, or bureaucratism. But in doing so, it clearly underestimates the role played by Stalin himself and his supporters. This is discussed in Case Study 4. In contrast, the personalist explanation gives far too much weight to Stalin. It exaggerates the power he possessed and underestimates the role of other factors, especially his supporters throughout the political structure. The contextual explanation is flawed to the extent that it is deterministic. A context can only help define alternatives, it cannot decide which of those alternatives will be adopted. In this sense, the context could not ensure that the Stalinist regime emerged, although it could make it more likely.

Stabilisation of the Stalinist Regime

The question remains of the link between October, Lenin and Stalin. The Leninist regime was clearly in part a response to the circumstances which existed in the immediate aftermath of the Revolution. Under attack from outside and wishing to build an industrial power in a peasant country, resort to a centralised politico-economic structure was a rational response. When Lenin died there was no guarantee that the authoritarian features of the system would be maintained into the future. That those features were maintained and even strengthened was a matter of political choice. This choice was made principally by the political elite, of which Stalin was a member, but also seems to have been widely supported at the lower levels of the political structure. In this sense, the closure of the regime during the 1920s was a function of positive decisions taken in the context of the elite conflict characteristic of that decade.

The real contours of the Soviet system were laid at the time of the great transformation at the end of the 1920s–early 1930s. As discussion in chapter 4 shows, agricultural collectivisation and rapid industrialisation were not the only courses of development possible. The Right Opposition was suggesting another set of policies, which ultimately was rejected by political decision-makers. Similarly, the Great Terror did not grow naturally out of the conditions of the 1930s. Decisions had to be made to mount the Terror; the trials and arrests could not develop in the absence of political will.

This means that the main features of the Soviet regime were the product of political decisions taken at various times in the life of that regime. Stalin was important in the making of those decisions, but he did not do it alone. Once we accept that Soviet developments were the result of political decisions made by leading figures, arguments about the inevitable development of Stalinism fall away. If decisions were made which contributed to the building

On Stalin's death, his body was placed in Lenin's mausoleum on Red Square. In 1960, his body was removed and buried beneath the Kremlin wall. The top picture shows the mausoleum while Stalin's body lay next to that of Lenin. The lower picture shows the mausoleum after his body was removed (Sud Deutscher Verlag)

of Stalinism, alternative decisions could have been made which would have inhibited such a development. When independent actors have a part in the explanation, notions of inevitability cannot apply.

Of course, these actors did not act in a vacuum. The Leninist system did provide a basis upon which the Stalinist system could build. Organisational centralisation and the elimination of enemies created conditions conducive to the emergence of the Stalinist regime. But it did not make it inevitable. Stalinism may have been *a* logical extension of Leninism, but it was not the only one and was certainly not *the* logical extension of Leninism. This means that neither the October Revolution nor the Leninist regime had to finish in the Stalinist form the Soviet Union adopted in the 1930s.

WAS THE USSR A FAILURE?

The structure that Stalin built seemed solid and secure at the time of his death. But this solidity proved, in the long run, to be less sure than it appeared. Stalin's death created a crisis of power and authority within the system. The immediate crisis of power at the top of the regime was resolved by the elimination of the security apparatus as an institution independent of political control; the re-emergence of the Party as the leading body in the political system; and, by 1957, the emergence of Nikita Khrushchev as the leader. But the crisis of authority could not so easily be fixed.

The difficulty was that with Stalin's death, the main source of authority within the system and legitimacy of the system disappeared. This problem was increased by the destalinisation campaign Khrushchev launched in 1956. This campaign consisted of speeches (the main two were at the Twentieth Congress in 1956 and the Twenty-second Congress in 1961) in which the exaggerated image of Stalin was deflated. Khrushchev criticised Stalin's mistakes and blamed him for all problems in the USSR since 1934. This was accompanied by an attempt to remove the symbolism of Stalinism from Soviet society. All of Stalin's books were removed from libraries, his pictures were taken down, his statues removed, everything that had been named after him was renamed and, most important of all, his body was removed from the Lenin mausoleum where it had been placed following his death. But with Stalin thus denigrated, on what was the legitimacy of the system to rest?

The Khrushchev Period

Khrushchev sought to rest the legitimacy of the system on a number of different bases. The most important one was economic performance. Khrushchev promised that the USSR would outproduce the West and create a higher standard of living for communism than existed under capitalism. To this end, Khrushchev engaged in a variety of economic and organisational reforms designed to improve the functioning of the economy. But in 1964, with the economy still performing satisfactorily, Khrushchev was toppled from power. His flamboyant leadership style and his failure to establish his own power and authority within the regime left him vulnerable to attack. His political enemies organised a peaceful coup, and he was sent into retirement.

Bust placed over the grave of Stalin in 1971 (UPI/Bettmann)

The Brezhnev Period

Khrushchev was replaced as leader by two main figures, Leonid Brezhnev who became Party leader, and Alexei Kosygin, who became prime minister. Brezhnev soon asserted his dominance and became the leading figure in the regime until his death in 1982. The post-Khrushchev leadership adopted a much more conservative outlook than their predecessor. They clamped down on desta-linisation, stopping the criticism of Stalin and his period and even placing a bust over Stalin's grave. There were rumours that the Brezhnev leadership even intended to rehabilitate Stalin fully, although this did not happen. In other spheres, little attempt was made at reform, and many conservative measures were introduced. This was particularly important in the economic sphere, where an early attempt at decentralising reform (in 1965) was blunted. Following 1968, little effort was made to bring about economic change.

The collapse of the attempted coup in August 1991 was the trigger for the dissolution of the USSR. Power and authority in Moscow shifted from Soviet President Gorbachev to Russian President Boris Yeltsin (AAP Photo Library)

This may not have mattered if the economy had continued to perform well, but during the Brezhnev period the economy suffered a major decline. The command economy established by Stalin had been excellent at meeting major challenges like that posed by the early stages of industrialisation and the war when what was necessary was the mass production of standard items. It was less well suited, however, to meeting consumer demands with the variety that that implied. In the 1970s consumer demand grew, and it was becoming increasingly less well catered for by the economy. Furthermore, major investment decisions were continually postponed, with the result that the upgrading of plant and facilities that was needed was not carried out. This coincided with an economic downturn in the world economy and the need for the Soviet economy to rely heavily on more expensive sources of power. The economy ceased to grow, and even began to contract.

The Gorbachev Period

This was the situation that confronted Mikhail Gorbachev when he came to power in March 1985, following the two short-term leaders Andropov and Chernenko. Gorbachev tried to deal with this situation first by limited measures of reform then by a more radical reform. He found that he could not restrict the reform measures to the economy alone, and had to accompany this by wide-ranging political reform. But he was unable to retain control of this process, and as popular disillusionment with the Party and the regime became increasingly open, both the Party's power and authority were rejected. With both of these foundations of the structure removed, the Soviet system collapsed under the weight of a bungled coup in August 1991. At the end of the year, the Soviet Union was formally dissolved.

This means that the ultimate failure of the system was that it could not do what is essential to all systems, continue to reproduce itself. The structure, established in its essentials by Stalin, could not cope with the combination of systemic problems stemming from the single command structure and the mistakes of successive leaders. In this sense, the system failed. It remains to be seen whether a better form can be produced from its wreckage.

BIOGRAPHIES

Beria, Lavrenty (1899–1953) Party and police positions in Georgia in 1920s and 1930s. Replaced Ezhov as head of security forces (NKVD) in 1938 and oversaw winding down of the Terror. Became a deputy premier after the war, but arrested and shot three months after Stalin's death.

Brezhnev, Leonid (1906–82) Held a succession of Party and government posts before succeeding Khrushchev as party leader in 1964. Presided over beginnings of Soviet economic decline.

Bubnov, Andrei (1883–1940) Revolutionary activist and later member of the Left Communist and Democratic Centralist oppositions. Later a Party and state official, arrested in 1937.

Bukharin, Nikolai (1888–1938) Revolutionary activist and theorist. Member of Left Communists, then later in 1920s opponent of Stalin. Defeated at end of 1920s. Arrested, tried and executed in 1938.

Bulganin, Nikolai (1895–1975) Economic administrator in 1920s, followed by a series of government posts. High Party and military posts during the war, Minister of Defence after it. Became premier in 1955.

Dzerzhinsky, Felix (1877–1926) Polish revolutionary who became the first chairman of the Soviet security apparatus, the Cheka, in 1918.

Ezhov, Nikolai (1895–1939) Political duties in the army during the Civil War, then a variety of Party posts. In 1936 replaced Yagoda as head of security forces (NKVD) and oversaw the height of the Terror. Removed in 1938.

Kalinin, Mikhail (1875–1946) Revolutionary activist from a peasant family. Effective president of the country following the death of Sverdlov in 1919.

Kamenev, Lev (1883–1936) Real name Rosenfeld. Jewish. Revolutionary activist, opposed to timing of October seizure of power. Opposed Trotsky and then Stalin during the 1920s, defeated by Stalin and removed from leading positions. Arrested in 1935, put on trial and executed in 1936.

Kerensky, Alexander (1881–1970)   A member of the Labour (Trudovik) Party and the State Duma prior to the Revolution. At the time of the February Revolution, he became a member of the Socialist Revolutionary Party and was elected to the executive body of the Petrograd Soviet. Served in the first Provisional Government as justice minister and war minister in the first coalition government. Prime Minister from the middle of the year until October, when he escaped into exile in the West.

Khrushchev, Nikita (1894–1971)   Held a succession of Party and government posts in Ukraine and Moscow. Supporter of Stalin. Succeeded Stalin as party leader, later combining this post with premier. Condemned Stalin and led destalinisation campaign.

Kirov, Sergei (1886–1934)   Real name Kostrikov. Revolutionary activist in the Caucasus. He was Party leader in Leningrad from 1925, replacing Zinoviev in this, and a firm Stalin supporter. A member of leading Party bodies, he was assassinated in 1934.

Kollontai, Alexandra (1872–1952)   Revolutionary and feminist who was a leader of the Workers' Opposition. Held a series of government, Party and diplomatic posts.

Kornilov, General Lavr (1870–1918)   Following a long army career, Kornilov was made Supreme Commander-in-Chief on 18 July 1917. He led his troops on a march towards the capital in August (the Kornilov affair), but they were disarmed and disintegrated en route. Following the October Revolution, he commanded one of the White armies, and was killed in action in April 1918.

Kosygin, Alexei (1904–80)   Held a series of industrial, administrative and government positions before replacing Khrushchev as premier in 1964. Presided over a period of economic decline before being replaced as prime minister a few months before his death.

Lenin, Vladimir (1870–1924)   Real name Ulyanov. Revolutionary activist, one of the founders of the Russian Marxist movement, and the founder and moving spirit of the Bolsheviks. Returned to Russia in April 1917, and played a major role in the October Revolution. First prime minister of the new Soviet state, he was clearly the dominant figure and main leader of both the Party and the government. Highly venerated after his death in 1924.

Lomov, Georgii (1888–1938)   Revolutionary activist, working in Moscow in 1917. A Left Communist in 1918, he later worked in economic administration. Arrested in 1937.

Lvov, Prince Georgii (1861–1925)   Born into one of the noblest families of Russia, Lvov was active in the local government (*zemstvo*) movement and the Progressive Bloc in the pre-1917 period. He was prime minister of the first Provisional Government which lasted until early May, and the following first coalition government. He resigned on 4 July 1917. Arrested after October, he escaped into exile in Paris.

Martov, Iulii (1873–1923)   Jewish. Important figure in early Russian social democracy, leader of Mensheviks after the split in 1903. Went abroad in 1920 following the failure of his more moderate line.

Miliutin, Vladimir (1884–1938)   Revolutionary activist, member of first Bolshevik government who resigned in protest at its all-Bolshevik composition. Later an economic administrator.

Molotov, Vyacheslav (1890–1986)   Real name Scriabin. Revolutionary activist, leader (along with Stalin) of Bolsheviks in Petrograd immediately after the fall of the tsar. Member of Politburo from 1926, prime minister from 1930–41 and commissar of foreign affairs 1939–49. Firm supporter of Stalin.

Nicholas II (1868–1918)   Last of the family of Romanov tsars. He ruled Russia from 1894 until March 1917. He and his family were taken captive by the Bolsheviks and executed on 17 July 1918.

Nogin, Viktor (1878–1924)   Revolutionary activist in Moscow in 1917. Resigned from the first Bolshevik government because of its all-Bolshevik composition. Later held a variety of posts in the Bolshevik government, before dying as a result of complications during an operation.

Plekhanov, Georgii (1856–1918)   Early Russian Marxist, mentor and then opponent of Lenin. An important figure in the introduction of Marxism to Russia.

Preobrazhensky, Evgenii (1886–1937)   Revolutionary activist and Left Communist. Wrote an important book with Bukharin about War Communism. Later held a series of government positions.

Pyatakov, Yuri (1890–1937)   Revolutionary activist, who first supported Trotsky in early 1920s and then crossed to Stalin. Senior positions in economic administration. Arrested, tried and executed in 1937.

Rasputin, Grigorii (1872–1916)   Russian holy man who gained influence at the court as a result of his apparent powers to halt the bleeding of the tsar's haemophiliac son, Alexei. He scandalised much of Russian society, and his role at the court helped to discredit the monarchy during the war. Killed in December 1916.

Rykov, Alexei (1881–1938)   Revolutionary activist, after October a leading economic official and prime minister from 1924–29. Supporter of Bukharin, and defeated by Stalin at the end of the 1920s. Arrested, tried and executed in 1938.

Shliapnikov, Alexander (1885–1937)   Revolutionary activist and worker Bolshevik, he was prominent in the Workers' Opposition in 1920. He remained around Party opposition circles throughout the 1920s, opposed to the growing control of the Party apparatus, and was expelled from the Party in 1933. He was arrested and executed in 1937.

Smilga, Ivar (1892–1937)   Lithuanian revolutionary activist who played an important organising role in the October Revolution. Later became an economic administrator. Arrested in 1932.

Stalin, Joseph (1879–1953) Real name Djugashvili. Georgian. Revolutionary activist, mainly in the Caucasus. Leader (along with Molotov) of Bolsheviks in Petrograd immediately after the fall of the tsar, eclipsed when Lenin returned. Had a series of government jobs after October, but most important appointment was as General Secretary in 1922. Defeated rivals in intra-party conflict during 1920s, consolidated his superiority in 1930s, including through the Terror. War leader, and unquestioned post-war dictator.

Stolypin, Pyotr (1862–1911) As governor of Saratov Province, he vigorously put down the 1905 peasant disturbances, and was subsequently promoted to minister of the interior and premier. Introduced significant land reforms as well as measures in other areas, and oversaw the imposition of restrictions on the Duma. Assassinated on 1 September 1911.

Sverdlov, Yakov (1885–1919) Revolutionary activist and Party administrator. First post-October leader of the All-Russian Central Executive Committee and chief secretary of the Party.

Tomsky, Mikhail (1880–1936) Real name Efremov. Revolutionary activist and trade union organiser. Member of the Right Opposition at the end of the 1920s. Committed suicide in 1936.

Trotsky, Leon (1879–1940) Real name Bronstein. Jewish. Revolutionary activist, chairman of Petrograd Soviet in 1905. On fringe of Menshevik party; joined Bolsheviks in 1917 and played a major organisational role in the October Revolution. Held successive government positions. Defeated by Stalin in mid-1920s, sent into exile in 1928, deported in 1929, and killed by one of Stalin's agents in 1940.

Uritsky, Moisei (1873–1918) Jewish. Revolutionary activist and leading Left Communist. Resigned over Brest-Litovsk. Assassinated in August 1918.

Voroshilov, Kliment (1881–1969) Military leader in Civil War, replaced Trotsky as commissar for defence in 1925. Stalin supporter, unsuccessful military commander in the Great Patriotic War.

Witte, Sergei (1849–1915) Following a series of administrative posts, Witte was appointed minister of finance in 1893. As minister, he was responsible for stimulating the major spurt of economic development at the close of the nineteenth century. Appointed premier in 1905, Witte prepared the October Manifesto, but was dismissed in April 1906 as a result of rivalries within the court.

Yagoda, Genrikh (1891–1938) Revolutionary activist who joined the security forces (Cheka) at the end of the Civil War. In 1934 became head of those forces (now NKVD) and prepared the first of the trials. Later arrested, tried and executed.

Zinoviev, Grigorii (1883–1936) Real name Radomylsky. Jewish. Revolutionary activist, close to Lenin, although opposed Lenin's call for October seizure of power. Party leader in Petrograd/Leningrad until removed as a result of defeat by Stalin in mid-1920s. Arrested in 1935, put on trial and executed in 1936.

GLOSSARY

All-Russian Congress of Soviets In 1917, the national organisation to which lower level soviets sent representatives. It saw itself as an alternative to the Provisional Government. After October, the formal supreme parliament of the Soviet state. In 1936 became the Supreme Soviet.

Bolsheviks When the Russian Social Democratic Labour Party split in 1903, the majority faction was called the Bolsheviks. Led by Lenin, the Bolsheviks seized power in October 1917. The party went through successive name changes: Russian Communist Party (1918), All-Union Communist Party (Bolsheviks) (1925), and Communist Party of the Soviet Union (1952)

Central Committee (CC) Major leading organ of Communist Party. Formally elected by Party Congress; from 1919 elected Politburo and 'formed' Orgburo and Secretariat.

Central Rada First revolutionary government in Ukraine. It ruled from March 1917 until April 1918 and sought to gain Ukrainian independence from Russia.

Collective farms (kolkhozy) Agricultural units established through the policy of collectivisation. These were large farms which were worked collectively and managed centrally. Formally the peasants collectively owned the land and their income depended on its output. In practice, peasants had no effective ownership rights.

Collectivisation The policy introduced in 1929 of forcing all private peasant farmers into collective farms. It was accompanied by much suffering and death.

Command economy The sort of economy introduced by the Bolsheviks. Its main characteristic was that all decisions were made at the centre by the planning agency and passed down to the production units in the form of plans. There was, formally, no room for market forces. Also known as a planned or administered economy.

Communism   The political philosophy stemming from the work principally of Karl Marx and Frederick Engels. It involved a society in which there was no private ownership of the means of production, no classes and no state, with governmental affairs being run by all the citizenry. The avowed aim of the USSR.

Congress (Party)   Formally the supreme decision-making body of the Communist Party. Consisted of representatives of the rank-and-file Party members, adopted major decisions on policy and elected CC. Congresses held: 1898, 1903, 1905, 1906, 1907, 1917, 1918, 1919, 1920, 1921, 1922, 1923, 1924, 1925, 1927, 1929, 1930, 1934, 1939, 1952, 1956, 1959, 1961, 1966, 1971, 1976, 1981, 1986, 1990.

Constituent Assembly   In 1917 all revolutionary groups were agreed that a popularly elected Constituent Assembly should be convened to make the most important decisions about the Russian future. Election was held in November 1917 and it met only once in January before being disbanded by the Bolsheviks.

Constitutional Democratic Party (Kadets)   Organised in 1905 by progressive figures, this party played an important role in the pre-war State Duma. As a centrist party, it was sidelined by the radicalisation of the Revolution in 1917 and suppressed soon after the Bolsheviks came to power. Its most important leader was Pavel Miliukov.

Dual power   Name given to the relationship that existed between the Provisional Government and the Petrograd Soviet where the former did not have effective power without the support of the latter. Power was thus shared in an uneasy balance.

Duma   The State Duma was introduced as part of the October Manifesto in 1905. It was to be the lower house of a bicameral parliament (the upper house was the State Council). The first two Dumas were too oppositionist for the tsar and were dismissed after serving only a few months. Revised electoral procedures led to tamer assembles subsequently. A temporary committee of the State Duma gave birth to the Provisional Government in February 1917. Disappeared with October.

General Secretary   Post formed in the Communist Party in 1922 in an attempt to regularise its organisational affairs. Filled by Stalin, this became a major power centre in the Party structure. Effectively head of the CC Secretariat.

Kulaks   The Russian word for fist. Derogatory term for rich peasants. This became a general term of abuse for all who opposed collectivisation, whether they were rich or not.

Leninism   The name given to the doctrine that was based on the writings of Lenin. After Lenin's death in 1924, this doctrine became largely a ritualised set of formulae.

Marxism   The name given to the political theory that stemmed from the work of Karl Marx and Frederick Engels. It was the philosophical basis for the main part of the socialist movement in Russia, including the Bolsheviks.

Marxism-Leninism   The formal doctrine through which the Communist regime sought to legitimise itself and to guide its actions following Lenin's death. It became increasingly ritualised and reduced to standard formulae under Stalin.

Mensheviks   When the Russian Social Democratic Labour Party split in 1903, the minority faction was called the Mensheviks. Opposed the Bolsheviks, including Lenin's reworking of Marxism. In opposition after the October Revolution, they were squeezed out during the Civil War.

Military Revolutionary Committee   A committee formed by Trotsky in the Petrograd Soviet, which conducted the practical planning for the October seizure of power.

New Economic Policy (NEP)   Economic policy introduced in March 1921 to replace War Communism. It involved the passing of farms and factories back into private hands, the promotion of private trade, and the stabilisation and regularisation of the economy on the basis of market principles.

Octobrist Party   Formed by political moderates who sought to use the 1905 October Manifesto as a basis for rebuilding Russia. Played a prominent part in the State Duma, but sidelined by the radicalisation of the 1917 Revolution. Most important figure was Alexander Guchkov, who was minister of war in the first Provisional Government.

Orgburo   The Organisational Bureau was established in March 1919 to handle all the most important organisational questions for the party. It was effectively the head body of the party bureaucracy. Its membership was in practice decided by the Politburo. It was abolished in 1952.

Politburo   After its founding in March 1919, the Political Bureau was the chief decision-making organ in the Communist Party. Formally elected by the CC, actually co-opted by membership of Politburo itself.

Popular Socialist Party   Founded in 1906 as a right-wing splinter from the Socialist Revolutionary Party (PSR). It opposed the use of terror (PSR policy at the time) and favoured the creation of a mass socialist party. It gained representation in the second and third Provisional Governments, but was sidelined by the radicalisation of the Revolution. Suppressed following October.

Provisional Government   Government set up by the temporary committee of the State Duma in March 1917 and claiming authority throughout Russia. Formally it ruled until the Bolshevik seizure of power in October. There were actually five Provisional Governments. The first, headed by Prince Lvov, ruled from 3 March to 5 May and fell because of the crisis over policy toward Word War I. The second, which ruled from 5 May to 2 July, was also headed by Lvov. This was the first coalition government, including official representatives of the Petrograd Soviet Executive Committee, and fell as a result of the failure of the offensive and disagreements over domestic policy. The third ruled from 25 July to 27 August and was the second coalition government. Headed by Kerensky, this fell as a result of the Kornilov affair. The fourth was the so-called Directory which ruled from 1–27 September and was led by Kerensky. It was designed to hold power until democratic, socialist and working-class forces decided whether to allow socialists to enter the government. Their inability to decide this enabled Kerensky to form the fifth (third coalition) government which held office from 27 September until 25 October.

Reds Bolsheviks and their supporters.

Russian Social Democratic Labour Party The first major Marxist party in Russia, founded in 1898. It split into Bolshevik and Menshevik factions in 1903.

Secretariat The CC Secretariat was a committee of Party secretaries that was to oversee the implementation of decisions of the Orgburo. Personnel affairs were centred here, and it was therefore a major source of power. It superseded the Orgburo in 1952.

Socialism Seen by Soviet ideologues as the stage before communism. Formally the USSR was declared to have achieved socialism in 1936. Sometimes loosely used interchangeably with communism.

Socialist Revolutionary Party (PSR) Founded in 1901, this party claimed to represent the peasants. Its philosophy was an amalgam of Populism and Marxism, but it was always internally divided. A main competitor of the Bolsheviks, it participated in the Provisional Government, chiefly through Kerensky and Victor Chernov. It opposed the Bolshevik seizure of power, although one flank of it, the Left SRs, initially joined the Bolsheviks in government. They left in March 1918, following which both Right and Left SRs were suppressed.

Soviet Russian word for council. In 1905 and 1917, spontaneous organisations of workers, peasants and soldiers. After October, official legislative organs (parliaments) of the Soviet state.

Sovnarkom (Council of People's Commissars) The government organ created by the Bolsheviks in October 1917. It consisted of all government commissars or, after 1936 when it became the Council of Ministers, government ministers.

Stakhanovite movement Mid-1930s emulation campaign based on the exploits of a miner, Alexei Stakhanov, who greatly exceeded his labour norm (the amount of coal he was expected to mine in a shift). He was projected as a model for others to emulate and in that way to increase production.

Trotskyism Term of abuse used to condemn those who followed the ideas of Leon Trotsky. It came to be used indiscriminately to apply to all of those who opposed Stalin.

Tsar Emperor of Russia.

War Communism Policy implemented by the Bolsheviks from mid-1918 until March 1921. It involved compulsory delivery of grain to the state, nationalisation of industry, a ban on private trade, and a rationing system for food and consumer goods. Replaced by NEP.

War Industries Committees Bodies established in May 1915 to provide voluntary public assistance in the organisation of industry for the war effort.

Whites Name given to anti-Bolshevik forces during the Civil War.

BIBLIOGRAPHY

This bibliography is confined to some of the major books on various aspects of Russian/Soviet history. No attempt has been made to list any of the enormous journal literature.

Barber, John & Harrison, Mark, *The Soviet Home Front 1941-1945. A Social and Economic History of the USSR in World War II*, Longman, London, 1991.

Carr, E.H., *A History of Soviet Russia*, 9 Vols., Macmillan, London, 1953-71.

Carr, E.H., *The Russian Revolution: From Lenin to Stalin 1917-1929*, Macmillan, London, 1979.

Christian, David, *Power and Privilege: Russia and the Soviet Union in the 19th and 20th Centuries*, Pitman, Melbourne, 1986.

Cohen, Stephen F., *Bukharin and the Bolshevik Revolution*, Wildwood House, London, 1973.

Conquest, Robert, *The Great Terror. A Reassessment*, Oxford University Press, Oxford, 1990.

Conquest, Robert, *The Harvest of Sorrow. Soviet Collectivization and the Terror Famine*, Hutchinson, London, 1986.

Conquest, Robert, *Stalin and the Kirov Murder*, Oxford University Press, Oxford, 1989.

Daniels, Robert V., *Red October: The Bolshevik Revolution of 1917*, Secker & Warburg, London, 1968.

Deutscher, Isaac, *Stalin*, Penguin, Harmondsworth, 1970.

Djilas, Milovan, *Conversations with Stalin*, Penguin, Harmondsworth, 1969.

Dunmore, Timothy, *Soviet Politics, 1945-53*, Macmillan, London, 1984.

Dunmore, Timothy, *The Stalinist Command Economy*, Macmillan, London, 1980.

Erickson, John, *The Road to Berlin*, Weidenfeld & Nicolson, London, 1983.

Erickson, John, *The Road to Stalingrad*, Weidenfeld & Nicolson, London, 1975.

Frankel, Edith Rogovin, Frankel, Jonathan & Knei-paz, Baruch (eds), *Revolution in Russia. Reassessments of 1917*, Cambridge University Press, Cambridge, 1992.

Fitzpatrick, Sheila, *The Cultural Front: Power and Culture in Revolutionary Russia*, Cornell University Press, Ithaca, 1992.

Fitzpatrick, Sheila (ed.), *Cultural Revolution in Russia, 1928–1931*, Indiana University Press, Bloomington, 1978.

Fitzpatrick, Sheila, *The Russian Revolution*, Oxford University Press, Oxford, 1982.

Getty, J. Arch, *Origins of the Great Purges. The Soviet Communist Party Reconsidered, 1933–1938*, Cambridge University Press, Cambridge, 1985.

Geyer, Dietrich, *The Russian Revolution. Historical Problems and Perspectives*, trans. Bruce Little, Berg Publishers, Leamington Spa, 1987.

Gill, Graeme, *The Origins of the Stalinist Political System*, Cambridge University Press, Cambridge, 1990.

Gill, Graeme, *Stalinism*, Macmillan, London, 1990.

Gill, Graeme, *Peasants and Government in the Russian Revolution*, Macmillan, London, 1979.

Ginsburg, Evgenia, *Into the Whirlwind*, Collins, London, 1967.

Hahn, Werner, G., *Postwar Soviet Politics. The Fall of Zhdanov and the Defeat of Moderation, 1946–53*, Cornell University Press, Ithaca, 1982.

Harrison, Mark, *Soviet Planning in Peace and War 1938–1945*, Cambridge University Press, Cambridge, 1985.

Hasegawa, Tsuyoshi, *The February Revolution: Petrograd 1917*, University of Washington Press, Seattle and London, 1981.

Hosking, Geoffrey, *A History of the Soviet Union*, Fontana, London, 1985.

Kaiser, D. (ed.), *The Workers' Revolution in Russia: The View from Below*, Cambridge University Press, Cambridge, 1987.

Katkov, George, *Russia 1917. The February Revolution*, Longman, London, 1967.

Keep, J.L.H., *The Russian Revolution. A Study in Mass Mobilization*, Weidenfeld & Nicolson, London, 1976.

Kochan, Lionel, *Russia in Revolution*, Paladin, London, 1970.

Koenker, Diane, *Moscow Workers and the 1917 Revolution*, Princeton University Press, Princeton, 1981.

Koenker, Diane P., Rosenberg, William G. & Suny, Ronald Grigor (eds), *Party, State, and Society in the Russian Civil War*, Indiana University Press, Bloomington, 1989.

Lampert, Nick & Rittersporn, Gabor T. (eds), *Stalinism, its Nature and Aftermath*, Macmillan, London, 1992.

Lewin, Moshe, *The Making of the Soviet System*, Pantheon Books, New York, 1985.

Lewin, Moshe, *Russian Peasants and Soviet Power*, Allen & Unwin, London, 1968.

Malle, Silvana, *The Economic Organization of War Communism*, Cambridge University Press, Cambridge, 1985.

McCauley, Martin, *The Russian Revolution and the Soviet State 1917–21*, Macmillan, London, 1975.

McCauley, Martin, *The Soviet Union 1917–1991*, Longman, London, 1993.

McNeal, R.H. (ed.), *Resolutions and Decisions of the Communist Party of the Soviet Union*, 5 Vols., University of Toronto Press, Toronto, 1974–82.

Medvedev, Roy, *Let History Judge*, Oxford University Press, Oxford, 1989.

Nove, Alec, *An Economic History of the USSR*, Penguin, Harmondsworth, 1972.

Nove, Alec, *Stalinism and After*, George Allen & Unwin, London, 1981.

Pares, Sir Bernard, *The Fall of the Russian Monarchy*, Knopf, New York, 1939.

Pipes, Richard, *Revolutionary Russia: A Symposium*, Anchor Books, New York, 1969.

Pipes, Richard, *Russia Under the Old Regime*, Weidenfeld & Nicolson, London, 1974.

Pipes, Richard, *The Russian Revolution 1899–1919*, Knopf, New York, 1990.

Rigby, T.H., *Communist Party Membership in the USSR 1917–1967*, Princeton University Press, Princeton, 1967.

Rigby, T.H., *Stalin*, Prentice Hall, Englewood Cliffs, 1966.

Rigby, T.H., *The Stalin Dictatorship*, Sydney University Press, Sydney, 1968.

Rittersporn, Gabor Tamas, *Stalinist Simplifications and Soviet Complications. Social Tensions and Political Conflicts in the USSR 1933–1953*, Harwood Academic Publishers, Reading, 1991.

Schapiro, Leonard, *The Communist Party of the Soviet Union*, Methuen, London, 1970.

Schapiro, Leonard, *1917*, Penguin, Harmondsworth, 1985.

Service, Robert, *The Russian Revolution 1900–1927*, Macmillan, London, 1986.

Service, Robert (ed.), *Society and Politics in the Russian Revolution*, St Martins Press, London, 1992.

Siegelbaum, Lewis H., *Soviet State and Society Between Revolutions, 1918–1929*, Cambridge University Press, Cambridge, 1992.

Smith, S.A. *Red Petrograd. Revolution in the factories 1917–1918*, Cambridge University Press, Cambridge, 1983.

Solzhenitsyn, Alexander, *The Gulag Archipelago*, 3 Vols., Fontane, London, 1974–78.

Tucker, Robert C., *Stalin as Revolutionary 1879–1929*, Chatto & Windus, London, 1973.

Tucker, Robert C., *Stalin in Power. The Revolution from Above, 1928–1941*, W.W. Norton & Co., New York, 1990.

Von Laue, Theodore H., *Why Lenin? Why Stalin? A Reappraisal of the Russian Revolution, 1900–1930*, J.B. Lillincott & Co., Philadelphia and New York, 1964.

Ward, Chris, *Stalin's Russia*, Edward Arnold, London, 1993.

Werth, Alexander, *Russia at War, 1941–45*, Pan, London, 1965.

INDEX